Breakfast
at
Tiffany's

Breakfast at Tiffany's

The Official
50th Anniversary Companion

Sarah Gristwood

RIZZOLI
NEW YORK

New York Paris London Milan

CONTENTS

We say that "diamonds are forever," and it's true! *Les Diamants Sont Eternels*. And—why not?—*Breakfast at Tiffany's* too!

To evoke this film—to see it again, to find once more the wonderful Audrey, her face, her look—is always that same intense pleasure, that same *glamour*.

That spark of enjoyment which shines steadily out.

Sparkling Audrey, *magic* Audrey, *sublime* Audrey, *fascinating* Audrey. I stop there because words fail me. Just one more. *Eternal* Audrey.

HUBERT DE GIVENCHY

INTRODUCTION

"There is a magic about Fifth Avenue at this hour."
—opening script lines from *Breakfast at Tiffany's*

In the movie-making business, it's highly unusual that the first hour of the first day of shooting becomes the first scene of the film. But that's how it happened on *Breakfast at Tiffany's*—and that first hour was blessed. The script called for early morning solitude: "A moment of limbo as the street lamps fade in the face of the purple onrush of dawn." Solitude is rare in New York City at any hour of the day, but at 5AM on Sunday morning, October 2nd, 1960, as the cab sped up Fifth Avenue, there was one brief moment when, recalls director Blake Edwards, every car and every person seemed to melt away. "It was as if God said, 'I'm going to give you a break now, but for the rest of your career you're going to have to live off this one,'" he remembers.

The cab door opens. A girl gets out and goes over to gaze into the window of Tiffany's. The scene is only a second or two in screen time, but in fact more than two hours had passed during filming, as a *New York Herald Tribune* journalist reported:

> "The conversion of Tiffany's into a movie set began at 5:30PM Saturday when the store closed for the weekend. A ten-man crew worked until midnight constructing camera platforms, setting up lights and covering the hardwood aisles with rolls of brown wrapping paper to prevent scratches.
>
> At 7AM yesterday the job was continued. A half hour later Miss Hepburn, coffee container in one hand and a sugar twist in the other, stepped from a cab in a black evening gown and strolled past Tiffany's in the breakfast scene that explains the title."

This scene, of course, was to go down in movie history. We have just had our first glimpse of Holly Golightly.

The *Herald Tribune* wasn't the only paper represented there. The shooting of *Breakfast at Tiffany's* on the New York streets was big news, and everyone wanted to cover the story. A *New York Times* reporter, Eugene Archer, described Hepburn's nervousness, "reflected in a series of stubbed-out cigarettes." Her anxiety even spread to the camera crew, who filmed her from inside the window of the store. "Miss Hepburn, it developed, had no affection for the Danish [pastry], preferring ice cream at Schrafft's and even less enthusiasm for the gaping crowd," Archer wrote.

By this time, it was not only the reporters who were beginning to gather. That 5AM moment of peace and emptiness was never likely to be recreated as the morning really got underway. As the next few hours ticked by and the crew moved inside the store to shoot the wide opening shot of the later scene where Paul and Holly visit Tiffany's, a shifting crowd of more than twelve thousand spectators stopped to watch, controlled by forty security men, and a host of officers from the New York City Police Department. Hepburn admitted later that, coming fresh from the quiet of her home in Switzerland, she found the noise and confusion of Manhattan

difficult to take. But the sheer verve and energy of the New York scene would be an important element in the movie. Truman Capote once said that New York was "the most stimulating of all the cities in the world. It's like living inside an electric light bulb." Never more so than at this moment, maybe.

Eugene Archer speculated, only half jokingly, that the waiting crowds may even have been disappointed to see "nothing more" than Hepburn. They might have been expecting a jewel robber—or "a glimpse of Premier Khrushchev." Because this was an extraordinary time to be making a movie, and especially in New York City. In those autumn weeks, Russian President Nikita Khrushchev and new Cuban leader Fidel Castro were both in town for a meeting of the United Nations. Beyond the city, Richard Nixon was embarking on a series of televised presidential debates with John F. Kennedy; racial

PREVIOUS PAGE: The first glimpse of Hepburn, in her Givenchy gown, would prove the key image for the whole film. ABOVE: Filming took place alongside the U.S. presidential election. OPPOSITE: Hepburn and Peppard share a lighthearted embrace.

strife was growing in the southern states; there were the first rumbles of trouble in far away Vietnam. For better or worse, a new age was dawning—an age of romanticism and revolution, of Andy Warhol and the hippies. In the years ahead, a critic would joke to Hepburn that Holly Golightly could have ended up among the flower children. "Yes, look what I started," Hepburn said wryly.

In the opening shot of the film, she wears a black evening dress—an item of clothing that had been around for decades—but the suspension collar of Hubert de Givenchy's inspired design gives it an extraordinary modernity. It's a sophisticated game, a *double entendre* of a dress: deceptively plain from the front, bold and surprising from behind. Many pages of print have been devoted to the style of *Breakfast at Tiffany's*, and many of those have explored the significance of the Little Black Dress. It can be a blank canvas, onto which the wearer can trace her own personality. Holly has chosen to accessorize it with ropes of fabulous fake pearls, clasped with diamante, that almost weigh down her slender neck as she gazes at the real jewels in Tiffany's window.

The huge sunglasses that obscure her eyes render her face almost expressionless, and already we sense that may be why Holly wears them—that there are experiences in her life from which she would prefer to hide away. Though she is dressed for an evening date, she is strolling the streets in the small hours of the morning, alone. Around the same time that *Breakfast at Tiffany's* was being filmed, author/journalist Joan Didion wrote a feature detailing this new kind of woman. New York City, she wrote, was the natural home for girls "who want to prolong the period when they can experiment, mess around, make mistakes. In New York there is no gentle pressure for them to marry." As Holly looks unsmilingly into Tiffany's window we sense that such choices may exact a price, but we also sense their inherent bravery. To many film critics who have felt

moved to judge it over the last half century, *Breakfast at Tiffany's* is a flawed picture, with its anomalies plain to see. To its legion of fans, on the other hand, it's a hymn to love and to loneliness—to sex and to style. What woman hasn't got a little black dress and pearls in her imagination? What woman can't hear the opening line of "Moon River" or "Golly, darling," spoken in Holly's clipped, eager way?

The question is: Why the movie's appeal is so enduring? If we examine the opening sequence, and the circumstances under which it was filmed, perhaps we may find the key. *Breakfast at Tiffany's* was made at a moment when the world was beginning to change—and change for women, in particular. If *Breakfast at Tiffany's* hadn't been so vividly of its own time, it would not have so seductive a magic today.

OPPOSITE: *Hepburn caught between takes.* BELOW:
In April 1961, while the film was still in post-production, Yuri Gagarin embarked on the first manned space flight.
OVERLEAF: *Shooting brought the New York traffic to a halt.*

PART ONE: SETTING UP

CHAPTER ONE
THE STORY

Who is Holly Golightly? According to the Paramount's press notes, the Holly Golightlys of the world can be found virtually anywhere, though she is not just *any* woman:

"It is possible, if you have looked in, however briefly, at some of the best bistros and great hotels of New York, San Francisco, Chicago, Los Angeles, London, Paris—or make it Cairo, if you like—it is possible that you have seen or met a girl like Holly Golightly. It is not only possible, it is probable, although the Holly Golightlys of this world are improbable girls to begin with. They come from anywhere, from Arizona and Azusa, Dubuque and Detroit, Brooklyn and Boston, or from Texas. They are pretty things. They are high-fashion things. They move swiftly and lightly in a circle of the best bars and the best bank accounts. They are what the *New York Times*, which is knowledgeable in these matters, calls 'Playgirls on the Town.' They are not necessarily as frisky as you might think. They are fun girls. They are fair but not necessarily *laissez-faire*."

And who better to create such a heroine than Truman Capote? According to Paramount, "Mr. Capote, a country boy to begin with, is a city man of ultra-sophistication now—just the imaginative reporter to bring a Holly alive, warmly breathing and coolly dashing in several directions at the same time." Except that the Holly Golightly of the movie is not quite the Holly Golightly Capote created.

Capote's hundred-page novella starts out with the writer/narrator—a character who, in the movie, becomes George Peppard—unable to let go of the question of what had happened to the girl named Holly. Is it true she had been spotted in Africa? This was, after all, a girl of whom almost anything was possible. A girl who, as the novella describes her, read only tabloids, travel folders, and astrological charts, "smoked an esoteric cigarette called Picayunes: survived on cottage cheese and melba toast," a girl whose "vari-colored hair" was "somewhat self induced."

PREVIOUS PAGE: *An iconic publicity shot taken in the New York studio of photographer Howell Conant.*
ABOVE: *Truman Capote in spring 1960 with heiress Gloria Vanderbilt, a friend from his boyhood and one of the many women associated with the character of Holly Golightly.*
OPPOSITE: *A last-minute conference on set.*

Capote's heroine was also a girl who, unlike the Holly of the movie, clearly slept with men for money. "I mean, you can't bang the guy and cash his cheques and at least not *try* to believe you love him," she says. The writer was a figure of anonymous personality (and unexplored sexuality), instead of George Peppard's muscular authority. There was no question of his proving himself as Holly's romantic hero—instead, he is just the ultimate outsider who desperately wants to be in. Not much like Peppard, but, perhaps, like Capote.

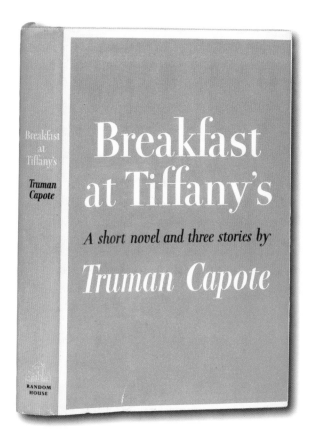

Truman Capote was thirty-five when *Breakfast at Tiffany's* came out, and already a celebrity. Born Truman Streckfus Persons in New Orleans, he had taken his stepfather's name, in preference to that of the father who had deserted him. That decision says something both about the indelible mark left by his trauma, and the capacity for self-invention he developed in response—not unlike his heroine Holly.

His debut novel, *Other Voices, Other Rooms,* had been hailed by New York's *Herald Tribune* as "the most exciting first novel by a young American in many years." Novelist and essayist William Styron called Capote "a man of almost unique talents;" W. Somerset Maugham, "the hope of modern literature." But it is typical of the tiny, angel-faced figure, who

was already becoming the *enfant terrible* of American literature, that even this warm reception had depressed him; in his mind, it fell short of the over-the-top adulation he'd achieved for his short stories. When it came to *Breakfast at Tiffany's*, the emotional and professional stakes were high for Capote to prove, if only to himself, that he was a literary giant.

In an early draft, the leading character was named Connie Gustafson, later changed to Holiday Golightly. The book's title came from one of those urban myths told at the expense of an out-of-towner—and one that reflects Capote's own open homosexuality. A marine was being "entertained" by a middle-aged New Yorker one Saturday night during World War II. The night went so well the man felt he should buy the marine a present, but since all the stores were closed on Sunday, he offered breakfast instead. "Pick the fanciest place in town," he said expansively. The marine dredged up the only grand name he knew—the place that had become a legend for sophistication—and said he wanted breakfast at Tiffany's.

The hundred-page work had had a troubled history. As far back as 1955, Capote had written to his then editor, Phyllis Cerf, that he hoped to have something interesting to show come September, but it wasn't until the spring of 1958 before the manuscript was finally handed over. Cerf (whose husband, Bennett Cerf, was co-founder of Random House, Capote's publisher) said she had read several versions and watched him struggle, as he had with other works before. "I think quite often the problem was that he hadn't thought of an ending, though he swore to me that I was wrong."

Breakfast at Tiffany's was to have been printed first in *Harper's Bazaar*, with book publication following very shortly after. The copy was submitted and was accepted. Alice Morris, *Harper's* fiction editor, recalled that even the layouts were done, focusing on Holly's eponymous Cat—"A cat in a window, mysterious-looking, slightly shady and misty." But as the piece was passed up the chain of command, letters began to filter down from senior executives. One thing Dick Deems objected to, for example, was the use of a four-letter word. "I used to get these lists of objections from either the publisher's office or the Hearst office across town," Morris recalled. "They all were reading as they had never read before, word for word."

She got the objections boiled down, and persuaded Capote to make the changes. The pages were ready to go to the printer and Capote was on his way to a long holiday in Greece, having first brought Morris a blue Tiffany box with a replica of a rose inside it, when Dick Deems declared they could not run the story, despite having paid additional money for the rights—almost three times the usual top fee. Another denizen of the magazine, Eleanor Perényi, recalled that it was actually editor Nancy Snow who pulled the story, afraid that Tiffany's, a major advertiser, would be unhappy about Holly's profession and Capote's language, as well as the bisexuality of Holly's friend Mag Wildwood. Morris tried to reassure them—Tiffany's would one day be proud to make the connection in their store window, she said prophetically, but in vain.

Esquire magazine heard what had happened and cabled Capote in Athens, offering to pay him $1,000 more. Money well spent, said *Esquire's* feature editor Clay Felker. "We ran it in the November issue. It had a dynamic effect on the sales," he said, especially after the novella also came out in book form, followed by wonderful reviews. Literary giant Norman Mailer wrote a little later that he would not have changed two words of the "small classic" that was *Breakfast at Tiffany's*. And, as for *Harper's*, once revered for its handling of fiction, after this, "I wouldn't spit on their street," Capote said.

Next came what Capote called "the Holly Golightly sweepstakes."

Everyone, it seemed, wanted to be known as the inspiration for Holly, all the more so since Capote was known for the strength of his female friendships and the group of beautiful and dynamic women he gathered around him. The pattern had begun in his teens when he had moved with his mother to Greenwich, Connecticut. It was there that he met

BELOW AND OVERLEAF: Carefully posed photographs, like the 1948 shot by Carl Von Vechten, helped build Capote's early fame.

his like-minded suburban exile, Phoebe Pierce (later Vreeland). The two of them would go to New York City and, defying the underage drinking laws, visited clubs like El Morocco and the Stork Club. They remained friends long after those days were passed. One of their mutual friends told Gerald Clarke, Capote's official biographer, that "as much as Truman could be in love with a woman, he was in love with Phoebe."

When he was eighteen, Capote and his mother moved to New York City, where he met Elinor Marcus, daughter of a former aviation executive and a Park Avenue princess, who introduced him to her sister Carol. Phoebe described Carol as "a licensed screwball." Carol, in turn, introduced him to her best friends, the heiress Gloria Vanderbilt and Oona O'Neill, daughter of the playwright Eugene. By fall 1944, as Capote turned twenty and became a full-time writer, Carol and Oona had gone to California—Carol to marry novelist and playwright William Saroyan and Oona, Charlie Chaplin. (Carol would later marry Walter Matthau, while Gloria married the conductor Leopold Stokowski.) It was the following year when his short stories made him the toast of the town overnight, and soon after that he found another playmate in the leggy blonde form of the good-time girl Doris Lilly. A one-line, one-picture starlet, she has been compared to the life-giving Rosie Driffield in W. Somerset Maugham's novel *Cakes and Ale*. She and Capote shared walks, ordered dinner in to her walk-up, and talked on the phone for hours.

Later a syndicated gossip columnist, and author of *How to Marry a Millionaire* and *How to Make Love in Five Languages*, Lilly recalled, "Pamela Drake and I were living in this brownstone walk-up on East Seventy-eighth Street, exactly the one in *Breakfast at Tiffany's*. Exactly. Truman used to come over all the time and watch me put make-up on before I went out . . . Truman was in the apartment a lot. There's an awful lot of me in Holly Golightly."

CAPOTE'S WORLD

"New York," Capote said, "is like a city made out of modeling clay. You can make it whatever you want." What he made of his life there was one long party—and everybody came.

From his earliest days as a literary lion he was able to flit from Anaïs Nin to Marlene Dietrich—a tiny, flamboyant figure beloved of hosts whose other guests had names like Maria Callas, Rudolf Nureyev, and Tennessee Williams. He pranced around Connecticut in beach clothes made for him by Schiaparelli, traveled in Russia with Cary Grant, and Japan with Cecil Beaton. When he went to Los Angeles he lunched with Joan Crawford and Greta Garbo; his intimates included Marilyn Monroe, Elizabeth Taylor, and Jacqueline Kennedy.

The party continued around the fashionable parts of the globe, from Tangier to Paris to Sicily—and yet, to many, his finest book is *In Cold Blood*. Published in 1966 (the study of two convicted murderers in unglamourous Kansas, a year-long project to which he committed himself absolutely), it became the subject of the acclaimed biopic starring Philip Seymour Hoffman as Capote.

But Capote's very passion for friendship was rooted in insecurity—the insecurity which ultimately allowed him to write the character of Holly Golightly. Phoebe Pierce Vreeland told George Plimpton of how eagerly he anticipated his estranged father's sending him a family ring, and his disappointment when it turned out to be something "like out of a Crackerjack box"—shades of the movie scene between Paul and Doc. She helped him sell it at one of the department stores, and they drank Manhattans with the money.

A small circle of friends would never be enough. He collected people avidly. Marella Agnelli, wife of the Fiat tycoon, admitted to the surprise of finding out that her closeness to Truman was far from exclusive—"Too many swans," she said. Many of those friends—even the famous "swans"—had abandoned him long before his final descent into drink and drugs.

In his youth, all the women he knew had wanted to claim some part in inspiring Holly Golightly. Less than twenty years later, when he parodied his society friends in another story, *La Côte Basque*, he found himself ostracized. *New York* magazine ran a cartoon on the cover of a French poodle causing havoc in a formal party. "Capote Bites the Hands That Fed Him," ran the caption. Capote himself professed to be taken aback by the reaction. "All a writer has for material is what he knows," he said. "At least, that's all I've got."

In the novella of *Breakfast at Tiffany's* he had dramatized the dilemma of the writer torn between observation and participation—of the outsider who wants desperately to be "in," but needs still to keep his outsider's freedom. His love had been given to a series of men throughout his life—as well as to his beloved bulldogs—but it was at the house of Joanne Carson, Johnny Carson's ex-wife, that he died in 1984 just before his sixtieth birthday.

Gerald Clarke reports that a mutual friend remembers Lilly yelling, "It's me! It's me! It's me!" when the book came out. When Capote was told of this, he said, "Honey, you tell her, her, her for me, me, me that it is her. But it's also Carol Marcus and Oona Chaplin." John Malcolm Brinnin, another friend and himself a biographer of Capote, was less sure: "We all knew girls somewhat like that but the difference was that [Holly] really was a kind of high-class hustler. The girls we knew might have been amused about sexual associations and so on, but they weren't into the big time like Holly."

Later in life, Capote also had the group of women he called his "swans," women with famous surnames and often-famous faces: Gloria Guinness, Pamela Churchill, Babe Paley, C. Z. Guest, Slim Keith, and Marella Agnelli. No one suggested these advantageously married aristocrats, a Who's Who of American society, were any model for Holly, a poor girl on the make. All the same, Clarke suggests they had something in common besides beauty, money and style, and that was a story, an ambition, a past. Capote said each—like Holly, surely—was an artist "whose sole creation was her perishable self."

But there are and will always be other candidates, notably the model sisters Dorian Leigh (whom Capote called "Happy-Go-Lucky") and Suzy Parker. Capote used to visit Leigh in her apartment by climbing up the fire escape, to be welcomed by her pet cats. Yet, not all the possible inspirations were flesh and blood: in *Playboy* in 1969, Gore Vidal, Capote's friend-turned-rival, accused him of having "abducted" Christopher Isherwood's Sally Bowles for the character. Novelist James A. Michener remembers that, in the 1950s, he and Capote both dated "a stunning would-be starlet-singer-actress-raconteur from the mines of Montana. She had a minimum talent, a maximum beauty, and a rowdy sense of humor. Also, she was six-feet, two-inches tall . . ."

When Capote's novella came out, and a New Yorker named Bonnie Golightly threatened to sue, Michener, in his youthful naïvete, wrote a well-intentioned letter to Capote's publisher at Random House, saying, of course, the claim was false since he, Michener, knew for sure the character of Holly Golightly was actually based on the Montana girl they both knew. The next thing he knew, the head of Random House was on the phone yelling at him to burn any copy of the letter . . . Capote had been afraid she was going to sue, too. In fact, with her height and her "bubbling charm," she sounds more like the Amazonian Mag Wildwood than Holly.

Bonnie Golightly charged Capote with invasion of privacy as well as libel, and sued for $800,000, but the case was quickly thrown out. "It's ridiculous for her to claim she is my Holly. I understand she's a large girl nearly forty years old. Why, it's sort of like Joan Crawford saying she's Lolita," Capote said indignantly. But many years later, the author Lawrence Grobel asked Capote whether Holly did, indeed, come from someone in real life. To which Capote, without detail, answered shortly: "Yes."

There might be elements in Holly of his damaged and damaging mother, Nina, the woman born "Lillie Mae" in the South, who shares with Holly (born Lulamae) a passion for New York, and a determined self-invention. Phoebe Pierce Vreeland described Nina to Gerald Clarke as a woman of two sides, the light and the dark, with the latter unleashed by alcohol. "The clue that she had been drinking too much was a kind of ominous, razor-edged gaiety," she said. Phoebe herself didn't think Capote had ever written about his mother, but concedes that her [Nina's] suicide in the early 1950s could not be other than a central experience in his life. In some ways, perhaps, Capote was himself the best inspiration for Holly. Where she had "the mean reds," he had panic attacks, and a final descent into drugs, alcohol, and ill-health he described as a "hard black rain."

Holly Golightly was a great role, a combination of darkness, girlishness, and glamour. But in the context of the times, to get it right would be a challenge. A few years down the line, Paramount's press notes for the finished movie would claim Capote "did not have Hepburn in mind, but he might have: Miss Hepburn, an internationalist, dotes on fun, and dotes on being a girl." The truth was far from that simple. There would soon be another sort of sweepstake going on—the quest for the actress to play Holly Golightly.

ABOVE: A different version of the snapshot Doc shows to Paul, with Holly in her earlier life as child bride Lulamae.

CHAPTER TWO
THE SCRIPT

The movie rights to *Breakfast at Tiffany's* were, says the movie's co-producer Martin Jurow, "one of the most coveted of properties." Events moved fast, the story was published in October 1958, and by April 1959 a first draft of the screenplay was already under discussion. Somewhere in there was the agreement with Truman Capote.

Everyone was after an option on the story, through the usual channels. But Martin Jurow, a former William Morris agent and Harvard Law School graduate, always believed in going directly to the source. He flew to New York "to meet with the imperious author," and later described the meeting at Capote's favorite Colony Club in his memoirs. Only Mae West, he writes, could have made a bigger production out of his entrance than did Capote, and over the next few hours, Jurow was only able to get in a few words, asserting his and his co-producer Richard Shepherd's urgent desire to make the movie "and our loyalty to his ideas regarding the story." This latter point, of course, would later be the source of some controversy. But, as Jurow recounts, another problem seemed more pressing:

"'You know, of course, that I want to play the male lead,' Capote said, tossing off the line in a manner too firm to be dismissed.

I stared. I gulped. Was he testing me? Was he playing games? No, he was absolutely serious. And he definitely thought he would be a logical choice.

I wrestled for a solution that would both stroke his ego and change his mind.

'Truman, the role just isn't good enough for you,' I said, recalling his delight when all eyes followed his grand entrance. 'All eyes will be on Holly Golightly through every frame of the picture. The male lead is just a pair of shoulders for Holly to lean on. You deserve something more dynamic, more colorful.'

He paused for an interminable moment. Then he said, 'You're right. I deserve something more dynamic.'"

BLAKE EDWARDS

There cannot ever have been much doubt that Edwards would wind up in the showbiz industry. Born William Blake Crump in 1922, he was the stepson of stage director and movie production manager Jack McEdwards, whose father was the silent film director J. Gordon Edwards. That earlier Edwards directed many of the movies of Theda Bara, the Cincinnati tailor's daughter reinvented as a French-Egyptian vamp and photographed surrounded by skulls and snakes.

The young Edwards started out as an actor with *Ten Gentlemen from West Point* in 1942 but when he also co-produced and co-wrote *Panhandle* six years later in 1948, it soon became apparent that his real talents lay behind the camera. In the early 1950s he began a successful collaboration with the director Richard Quine—with whom he wrote eight films, notably *My Sister Eileen* (1955)—and also attracted attention for his radio screenplays. But it was the end of the 1950s that suddenly saw him cast as the man of the moment—a director who could boast simultaneous triumphs on the big and small screen.

For television, he created the hit series *Peter Gunn* (1958–60), *Mr Lucky* (1959–60) and *Dante* (1960–61). In the cinema, he was beginning to make a name for himself with comedies like *Mister Cory* (1957) and *Operation Petticoat* (1959), both starring Tony Curtis. No wonder he seemed like the right man for *Breakfast at Tiffany's*—a director whose almost slapstick comedy could yet skirt more serious social satire, a man with his finger on the pulse of the changing times.

Nonetheless, *Breakfast at Tiffany's* represented a huge move up the ladder for Edwards, and its success carried him on to the years, and the films, that would prove the hallmark of his career. In 1962 came not only the tough thriller *Experiment in Terror* (1962), but also the moving *Days of Wine and Roses* (1962) with Jack Lemmon as an alcoholic PR man. Both films boasted music by *Breakfast at Tiffany's* composer Henry Mancini. And just a year later, in 1963, Edwards and Mancini teamed up again for *The Pink Panther* (1963)—the first film in a franchise still alive today.

There are critics who say that, ironically, the very success of the *Pink Panther* movies would prove to be something of a straightjacket for Edwards, who found himself typecast as the custodian of Inspector Clouseau. It's true that *The Great Race* in 1965 marked the start of a long series of disputes with the Hollywood studios. But alongside the *Pink Panther* sequels he continued to make other films as interesting, though not necessarily as successful. *The Party* in 1968 cast *Pink Panther* star Peter Sellers in a hilarious parody of a Hollywood gathering. In 1969 came *Darling Lili*, starring Julie Andrews, who married Edwards the same year.

Julie Andrews was again the star (and Henry Mancini the composer) of *Victor/Victoria* (1982), Edwards' admired comedy of sexual identity. Despite the box office success of *10* (1979), and the ongoing popularity of the *Pink Panther* franchise, his career never again attained the heights of the early 1960s, but (along, now, with several of his children) he has never ceased to play an active role in the film industry.

They met the next day in Capote's agent's office. Jurow knew Capote needed money, not least to decorate his home in the Hamptons. A price of $50,000—to Capote's delight—was agreed. Then Jurow made an extraordinary gesture "that granted me Truman's complete appreciation, however temporary that proved to be." He offered another $15,000, taking the total up to "then-princely" $65,000; later, he heard Capote was unhappy that he did not also get "points." As soon as the producers had optioned the rights to *Breakfast at Tiffany's*, they had set about developing the script. But there is a reason that the process is described by Shepherd as "development hell."

The producers initially commissioned a treatment from the Australian-born playwright Sumner Locke Elliott. It was, Shepherd would admit, a misguided attempt to get a script on "a more economical basis." The attempt failed—Elliott, noted for his TV drama and his novels, was less attuned to the big-screen culture, and, perhaps, not wholehearted enough in his commitment to turning the relationship Capote created into a Hollywood love story. A lengthy letter from Shepherd to Paramount executive Frank Freeman, dated April 16, 1959, makes it clear what the producers felt was going wrong (overleaf).

An alternative had to be found, and a memo of May 13 gave a list of possible writers and their price on recent projects, from Robert Alan Arthur, who had just done *Warlock* (a $75,000 flat deal) and N. Richard Nash of *Porgy and Bess* (ditto). Neil Paterson doing *Room at the Top* had asked $50,000; the award-winning radio dramatist Norman Corwin was quoted at $2,500 per week; and Meade Roberts, Tennessee Williams's collaborator, only "$1,000 per week (approximately)." But the choice lighted on George Axelrod, a New Yorker then in his late thirties, a sometime playwright and producer who'd started out writing forty jokes a week for *Grand Ole Opry* and who, at this point, already had *The Seven Year Itch* (1955) and *Bus Stop* (1956) under his belt.

PREVIOUS PAGE AND ABOVE: *Director Blake Edwards was still in his thirties when he came to* Breakfast at Tiffany's, *and best known for his stylish television work.* OVERLEAF: *A letter from co-producer Richard Shepherd to a Paramount executive reflects the difficulties of bringing Capote's novella to the screen.*

April 16, 1959

TO: Y. FRANK FREEMAN

                    RE: "BREAKFAST AT TIFFANY'S"
                         Dramatic Treatment --
                         Sumner Locke Elliott

Dear Frank:

Enclosed is the dramatic outline by Sumner Locke Elliott on
"Breakfast at Tiffany's". Marty and I have delayed officially
turning this over to you until now in order to discuss it not
only amongst ourselves but with John Frankenheimer.

Suffice to say we are all immensely disappointed in Elliott's
efforts. Disregarding its length and its peculiar physical for-
mat, we are most disturbed by its eposodic, disjointed, fluffy
and even ephemeral tone. Elliott, to our way of thinking, has
seriously failed to capture the warmth, the zest, the humor, the
beauty and, more important, the basic heart and honesty that is
Holly Golightly. The young man he has written is petty and un-
attractive in character, borders on the effeminate, which we all
detest, and as in the case with Holly and the whole piece, is
almost totally devoid of the humor and contemporary flavor that
is absolutely vital for this picture.

Most important, however, a dramatically sound story line and point
of view is either non-existent or certainly not clear. Capote's
book provides a marvelously wonderful character study of a fascinating girl, surrounded by almost equally interesting people
and locale.

Our task has been and continues to be one of converting this
character study into a clear-cut dramatic story line with an
even clearer audience point of view.

We spent considerable time and effort in story conferences with
Elliott with the primary objective of making certain that the
dramatic line and point of view in his treatment would be clear.
Somehow, as is so unfortunately often the case, the result did not
equal the expectations.

All of us are convinced that we are correct in assuming that the
boy and girl get together at the end of our story, that Holly's
problem, which is the principal one, is in some way resolved through
the understanding, love and strength of the boy. This requires a
completely different kind of male character than has been given to
us by Elliott and a far more solid construction of the dramatic
elements of the piece.

We therefore are of the singular opinion that a different man should be put on the job. One with infinitely more experience in dramatic construction, with a contemporary understanding of these people to say nothing of an appreciation for comedy that is not so perfumed. Our gamble on Elliott in the hopes of getting a proper script on the more economical basis did not pay off. There is some consolation, however, in the fact that we protected ourselves with a proper cut-off period.

In examining the pool of more experienced writers who are shortly available, we have come up with at least the following candidates who merit our serious consideration: Betty Comden and Adolph Green, James Poe, Helen Deutsch, Charles Lederer, possibly John Michael Hayes, George Axelrod and Everett Freeman.

Among the others who might be right but are not immediately available are: Samuel Taylor, Julius Epstein, Harry Kurnitz, Ernest Lehman and Isobel Lennart. Also, Paul Osborn, the Kanins, John Patrick and Dorothy Kingsley.

We now must put this back on its proper track.

/s/ Richard Shepherd

RS:in

cc D. A. Doran
   Bernard Feins

c
 o
  p
   y

2 Copies of Script
and letter to
Holman 7/17/59
   by B. 7.
      (w)

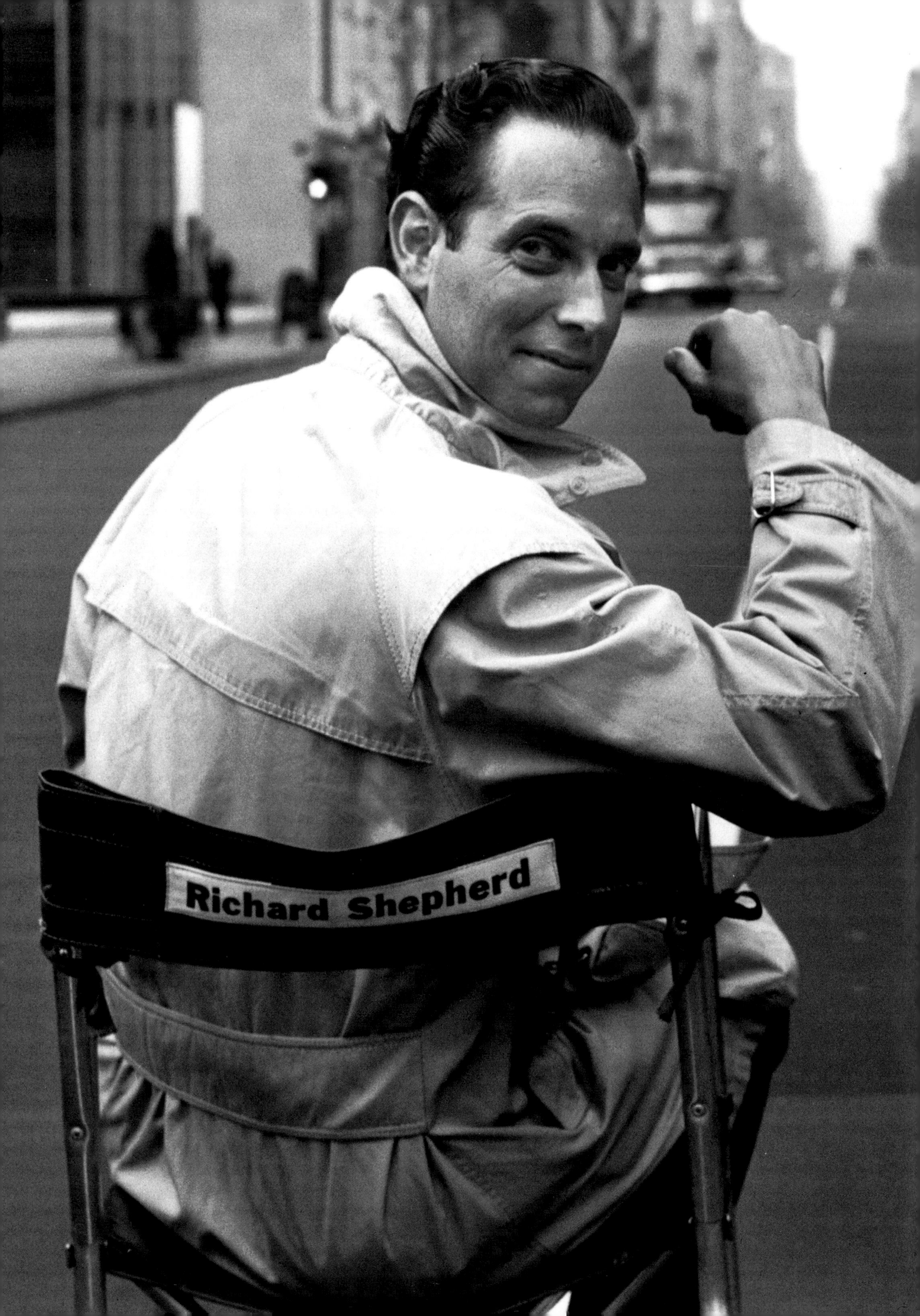
Richard Shepherd

In retrospect, Axelrod seems the obvious choice. Decades later, summing up his career, the *New York Times* would write that Axelrod's "sexually frank farces and feverishly witty satires of the fifties and sixties heralded the more cynical and hedonistic pop-culture sensibility of later decades . . . he was celebrated for a quirky, sophisticated sensibility that always seemed slightly ahead of the curve." But his involvement, like that of Hepburn, was far from being a given at first.

Axelrod's wife, Joan, had seen the novella before publication, when Capote had sent it to her in galley form. She showed it to her husband, George. Joan says, "He read it and said, 'What a fabulous character for a movie.' As very often happened with him, about two months later, at three o'clock in the morning, he woke up and said, 'I've got it! I know how to do *Breakfast at Tiffany's* as a movie.' He had the love story all worked out . . . because he was wise enough to the wicked ways of Hollywood to know that you had to do certain things."

As Joan Axelrod remembered it, "The people assigned to the movie told George they couldn't get him to do the script, because they needed a serious writer." Axelrod repeated this to his friend Capote, who supported him—whatever issues he might later have with the finished movie, and by implication, with Axelrod's screenplay. After the Elliott debacle, the producers came back to him and offered the proverbial "Rhode Island and a piece of the gross." Indeed, as a May 13 Paramount interoffice communication showed, Axelrod's agent, the legendary Swifty Lazar, was playing hardball, demanding $100,000 for screenplay and two sets of changes, to be done in twenty-six weeks.

Axelrod's input would be stretched out over a longer period by the fact his *Goodbye Charlie*, starring Lauren Bacall, was already scheduled to open on Broadway that fall of 1959. But, all the same, Jurow and Shepherd made it clear they wanted Axelrod, and

no-one else would do. The producers must have breathed a sigh of relief when, on May 15, Paramount got the magic telegram from Swifty Lazar:

PARAMOUNT PICTURES MARATHON AVE HOLLYWOOD (CALIF) UNDERSTAND PERFECTLY WE HAVE DEFINITE DEAL FOR AVELROD [sic] SUBJECT ONLY TO PARAMOUNT CONCLUDING DEAL WITH CAPOTE STOP MEANWHILE AVELROD [sic] COMMENCING WORK STOP LAZAR RETURNING MONDAY REGARDS LAZAR

With the script on the way, the producers could return to their other big challenge—casting the part of Holly.

ABOVE: *The signing of scriptwriter George Axelrod (pictured above in 1965), was central to the creation of the film we see today.* OPPOSITE: *Richard Shepherd on set.*

CHAPTER THREE
THE STAR

The part of Holly Golightly is now so closely associated with Hepburn, it is hard to imagine that it could have gone another way. Jane Fonda had been mooted, Shirley MacLaine was a desirable possibility but was already committed elsewhere, and someone at Paramount was convinced Rosemary Clooney would be perfect. By the late 1950s, moreover, Truman Capote's famous stable of female friends included Marilyn Monroe as well as Elizabeth Taylor. And Capote saw Monroe in the part.

At the time, Monroe was moving away from Hollywood, deep under the influence of her marriage to Arthur Miller. She was experimenting with the Method school of acting as popularized by Lee Strasberg, by which an actor seeks to find "theatrical truth" by analyzing a character's psychological motives and making a personal identification with them. It was also during this time that Monroe's problems with drugs and alcohol were surfacing. As *Breakfast at Tiffany's* went into production, Monroe was hospitalized from the set of *The Misfits* (1961), dabbling dangerously in alcohol and sleeping pills. But, perhaps, it was that combination of influences that appealed to Capote.

"Marilyn would have been absolutely marvelous in it," Capote would say later. "She wanted to play it, too, to the extent that she worked up two whole scenes all by herself and did them for me. She was terrifically good, but Paramount double-crossed me in every conceivable way and cast Audrey. The book was really rather bitter, and Holly Golightly was *real*—a tough character, not an Audrey Hepburn type at all. Holly had to have something touching about her—unfinished. Marilyn had that. Audrey is an old friend and one of my favorite people but she was just wrong for that part."

THIS PROOF IS
UNRETOUCHED

Martin Jurow recalls the situation differently. He would later tell a tale about flying back west from his all-important New York meeting with Capote, and finding a "vague and disoriented" Marilyn Monroe in the seat next to him. She had heard of "this Holly Golightly person" from her "feeders," photographer Milton Greene and acting coach Paula, wife of Lee Strasberg. But by the time the plane landed, Jurow was unsure Monroe—after several more drinks—"even knew what *Breakfast at Tiffany's* was." On the one hand, Jurow had felt that her casting would be too obvious, yet, at that moment, he saw Monroe herself in the terms used to describe Holly—"a phony. But a real phony." He was confused about his reactions—and about hers. (An additional complication was that co-producer Richard Shepherd had represented Marilyn Monroe in his William Morris days.)

But "Marilyn was kind of obvious. We thought we could do better," Shepherd would say years after the event. And a day or two later the question became irrelevant, when they had a call from Paula Strasberg, who declared, "There is no way she will play that girl. Marilyn Monroe will not play a call girl, a lady of the evening."

Strasberg's comments echoed the initial reactions of Hepburn and the people around her. No-one thought Hepburn would play a girl of such ambiguous morality—she had, after all, just turned down a part in Hitchcock's *The Hanging Judge* (1958) because the character suffered rape.

"Paramount didn't think she would play it because she was such a sweet, proprietary sort of lady," Shepherd says. Blake Edwards agrees. "I don't think the majority of audiences in those days really ever thought of Audrey Hepburn as a hooker, a call girl," he said. "And I bet even after the movie, most of them don't quite realize exactly what Holly does." But then Jurow and Shepherd themselves "had

never visualized Holly as a call girl. She was a woman who defied definition." And so—despite the Paramount's bosses telling them they had "no chance" with Hepburn—they would not give up.

PAGE 38: Hepburn between shots on the steps of Holly's brownstone. PREVIOUS PAGE: The marks on the left-hand image show how the publicity photograph of Hepburn was retouched before being released. The retouching is evidently minimal. ABOVE: Hepburn preparing for the 1954 Oscar ceremony at which she received a Best Actress award for Roman Holiday. *OPPOSITE: Hepburn in 1953 at a "Welcome Home" party at Claridges Hotel in London.*

The path to Hepburn was guarded by her "ferocious" agent Kurt Frings—the former boxer shared Paula Strasberg's views on his client playing what he, too, saw as a call girl. Moreover, he had a list of the eminent directors—namely William Wyler, Billy Wilder, George Cukor, and Joseph Mankiewicz— with whom he considered Hepburn safe. Blake Edwards, still known chiefly as a screenwriter and TV director, was not on that list. At last, after a stream of pleading calls, Frings agreed Jurow should be allowed to fly to Europe and talk to Hepburn herself.

When Jurow arrived, Hepburn greeted him warmly. "Oh, Martin, you have a wonderful script. But I cannot play a veritable hooker." As Jurow tells it, he played his ace. Rising to his full height, he declared with all the indignation of a Rex Harrison in *My Fair Lady* (1964) that if Hepburn did not know the difference between a hooker and "a dreamer of dreams, a lopsided romantic," they didn't want her near the movie anyway. With tears running down her face she said to him, "Oh, Martin, Martin, it will be all right." And, of course, it was. "Much, much, more than merely all right," as Jurow says fondly.

Hepburn was, after all, the actress who could get away with anything. She had appeared on stage in *Ondine* in a fishnet costume that created the impression she was virtually naked, and no-one had complained, because of . . . what? Her innate classiness? Her vulnerability? Her Europeanness? As Billy Wilder (Hepburn's director on *Sabrina* in 1954 and *Love in the Afternoon* in 1957) said of her, "She drew [the audience] in. She could say something risqué, but the way she did it had a kind of elegance that you could not, under any circumstance, mistake."

All the same, she was careful to stay behind a clearly defined line. In none of her roles had there been anything remotely resembling a sex scene, not even when she had played that other potential courtesan, Gigi. She had been seen in love, but never in lust.

But now, in the dawn of a new decade, Hepburn knew, according to her biographer Alexander Walker, she needed a movie "that would speed her transition to roles with a newer take on [sexual] morality." If the movie needed her, it's equally true she needed the movie.

Hepburn would try to rationalize Holly by recalling her own early days in cabaret. "She was caught off base. Lost. But she was pretending just as conscientiously as I did," Hepburn would say in an interview with trusted interviewer Henry Gris. This was very much the line the production would take: Shepherd would stress that Holly was "very sweet under the surface . . . The girl who gets fifty dollars to go to the powder room wasn't really the character Truman wrote." As Holly tells Paul in the script: "Look, I know what you think. And I don't blame you, I've always thrown out such a jazzy line. But really except for Doc . . . and yourself . . . José is my first non-rat romance."

When the movie was shooting in New York City, *New York Times* journalist Eugene Archer described a conversation with Hepburn, the "charming and lady-like" young actress who "seemed totally unlike the exhibitionist heroine she was determined to capture on film."

"It's true we've left the sex ambiguous in the script," he reported her as saying. "Too many people think of Holly as a tramp, when actually she's just putting on an act for shock effect, because she's very young." The journalist also reported that Hepburn, in character, would play a drunk scene, steal a five-and-dime-store Halloween mask, "and innocently share a bed with her leading man." For Hepburn to do any of these things was obviously newsworthy.

OPPOSITE: *Hepburn in the uncharacteristically revealing costume she wore for* Ondine, *the play she did with Ferrer in 1954.*

Hepburn once said she had been "luckier" than Holly in that her life had more purpose. She might have been speaking of her commitment to finding marriage and children, of her religious faith—or of her career. But she had sympathy for a girl who was making do with whatever scraps of love and luck the world would offer her. "If you pass the man with the canapés more often than usual, you may get yourself a kind of meal," she added.

She told Eugene Archer that she had hesitated a long time before accepting the part. "It's very difficult and I didn't think I was right for it. You know, I've had

very little experience, really, and I have no technique for doing things I'm unsuited to. I have to operate entirely on instinct. It was Blake Edwards who finally persuaded me. He, at least, is perfectly cast as a director, and I discovered his approach emphasizes the same sort of spontaneity as my own." Flying to her home in Switzerland, Edwards joined Hepburn's husband, her agent, and even her mother in convincing her that the style he used to shoot the picture would effectively purify the part.

Some doubts still remained. When the *New York Times* ran a second story about the movie on June 16, 1961, Hepburn told Murray Schumach, "I was terribly afraid I was not right for the part. I thought I lacked the right sense of comedy. This part called for an extroverted character. I am an introvert. But everyone pressed me to do it. So I did. I suffered through it all. I lost weight. Very often when I was doing the part, I was convinced I was not doing the best job."

But years later, looking back, she would acknowledge that playing Holly Golightly had been "a real revolution for me. After so many movies, I no longer felt like an amateur actress; I knew I'd always have something to learn, but I also discovered that I could give something of myself. I knew this role would be a challenge, but I wanted to tackle it."

Breakfast at Tiffany's, Hepburn said once, "was the best thing I've ever done because it was the hardest." By 1960, she had come a long way since arriving in America less than a decade before— Patricia Neal, meeting her on the set of *Breakfast at Tiffany's*, described her as the "queen of Hollywood." Now, perhaps she sensed the need for a new challenge. She was still, and always would be,

LEFT: *Hepburn photographed by Howell Conant for* Breakfast at Tiffany's *publicity, and* (RIGHT AND OVERLEAF) *waiting to be called on set.*

someone who needed a sense of safety—but if she took this role, she would be pushing her own personal boundaries.

* * * * * * *

Anyone who has watched *Breakfast at Tiffany's* has seen the first line of his new story emerge from Paul Varjak's typewriter: *There was once a very lovely, very frightened girl . . .*

But the words Truman Capote, and George Axelrod after him, applied to Holly Golightly could equally have applied to Hepburn. For despite the polished poise of her screen appearance—the elegance and apparent assurance of the thirty-one-year-old star she had become—Hepburn had grown up under conditions every bit as harsh as those Holly/Lulamae knew. And she, too, knew all about what Holly called "the mean reds." As Capote wrote:

> "The mean reds are horrible. You're afraid
> and you sweat like hell, but you don't know
> what you're afraid of. Except something
> bad is going to happen, only you don't know
> what it is."

Hepburn was born May 4, 1929, in Brussels of (mostly) Anglo-Irish and Dutch ancestry. Her mother's family was an aristocratic one, but her father's early desertion gave her what would prove an enduring insecurity: "All my personal relationships have been marked by that feeling of abandonment that has never left me." Part of her early childhood was spent in England, but in 1939 her mother took her back to the Netherlands, supposedly for safety from World War II—a disastrous decision. The Germans invaded Holland a year later, and her teenage years were spent suffering all the privations of an occupied territory.

Her life then must have seemed unimaginable, when she looked back from the days of her stardom. Anne Frank (extracts from whose diary Hepburn read at a UNICEF benefit concert in March 1990) was both a compatriot and an exact contemporary. "Anne Frank and I were born in the same year, lived in the same country, experienced the same war, except that she was locked up and I was on the outside. [Reading her diary] was like reading my own experiences from her point of view. I was quite destroyed by it," she said later. It's noteworthy, perhaps, that in Capote's original novella, *Breakfast at Tiffany's* was a wartime story.

Hepburn remembered her brothers eating dog biscuits, neighbors eating tulip bulbs, and bread that was green because it was made from ground peas. She weighed ninety pounds by the end of war, not nearly enough for her five-foot-seven-inch frame, and had jaundice and swollen feet. It's almost impossible not to think of the child Lulamae and her brother as Doc describes them in Capote's story: "Ribs sticking out everywhere, legs so puny they can't hardly stand, teeth wobbling so bad they can't chew mush." It's equally difficult not to think, too, of the UNICEF refugees to whom Hepburn's last years would be devoted.

In 1989, while visiting the Sudan, Hepburn saw a malnourished boy of fourteen. "He had acute anemia, respiratory problems, and edema (dropsy). And that was exactly the same way I finished the war." In her later career there would be media talk about how illogical it was to cast the elegant Hepburn as the disadvantaged characters of Eliza Doolittle and Holly Golightly, but, in fact, she was one of the few Hollywood actresses of her generation who did know what it was like to go hungry.

OPPOSITE: *A private photograph of Ferrer and Hepburn taken in 1956—one of their son Sean's favorites.*

Hepburn's wartime experience made her the person she would be. Robert Wolders, the companion of her last years, who had spent the war only ten miles away in Holland remembered agreeing with her that under those circumstances you "discover things that are quite exciting about oneself, in terms of loyalty to other people, the ability to have fun with very little. Your appreciation of life is honed, so any little thing is an encouragement, that life is really all right."

"I decided, very early on, just to accept life unconditionally," Hepburn said. "I never expected it to do anything special for me, yet, I seemed to accomplish far more than I had ever hoped. Most of the time it just happened to me without my ever seeking it." But as a child, her prospects looked far from sunny. The end of the war, when she was sixteen, brought not only a slow return to normality, but a return to England. Throughout the war years she had kept up her childhood dream of studying ballet, but when she came to audition for the famed Ballet Rambert, her height put her at a severe disadvantage. She found, too, she said, that she could no longer compete with girls who had had "five years of Sadler's Wells teaching, paid for by their families, and who had always had good food and bomb shelters."

Instead, she began picking up jobs around the fringes of the showbiz industry. "I was very ambitious and took every opportunity. I wanted to learn and I wanted to be seen." Her few movie parts were utterly unmemorable, among them *Monte Carlo Baby* (1951) which she accepted chiefly because it would take her to Monte Carlo—and it was there that the extraordinary break came that would change her life forever, in the unromantic setting of a hotel lobby.

As the legendary author Colette wrote after the event, "What author ever expects to see one of his brain-children appear suddenly in the flesh? Not I, and yet here it was! This unknown young woman,

English, I guessed, was my own thoroughly French Gigi come alive! That afternoon I offered her the part in the Broadway play."

It really was almost that fast . . . the stuff of sheerest fairy story. From nowhere and nothing, to a lead on Broadway, in the adaptation of Colette's novel *Gigi*. And the miracle did not end there. In a summer break from *Gigi* she flew to Italy to star opposite Gregory Peck as the truant princess in *Roman Holiday* (1953). By 1953, she was an international celebrity. A cover profile in *Time* quoted Billy Wilder, director of *Sabrina*, her next picture, as saying "Not since Garbo has there been anything like her, with the possible exception of Ingrid Bergman." *Breakfast at Tiffany's* was less than a decade away.

In 1954, as *Sabrina* was coming out, Cecil Beaton wrote a feature on Hepburn for *Vogue*, and left a vivid description: "A new type of beauty, huge mouth, flat Mongolian features, heavily painted eyes, a coconut coiffure, long nails without varnish, a wonderfully lithe figure, a long neck . . . In a flash, I discovered A. H. chock-a-block with sprite-like charm, and she has sort of waifish, poignant sympathy. Without any of the preliminaries I felt that she cut through to a basic understanding that makes people friends. Nothing had to be explained: we liked one another." *Sabrina* came out that year.

But there was another side to the staggering success story. To a reporter who asked Hepburn if she ever felt lonely: "When the chips are down, you are alone. That's the kind of loneliness that is terrifying. Fortunately, I've always had a chum I could call. And I love to be alone. It doesn't bother me one bit. I'm my own company, though I wouldn't want to be alone because nobody loves me or cares for me.

OPPOSITE: *The stage version of* Gigi *helped make Hepburn an instant celebrity.*

I can spend time happily alone because I know somebody is going to walk in the door. I'm rather cheerful by nature—it's my best defense against the aches on the inside."

In some ways, she seemed cool about her movie stardom, though suffering from terrifying stage—or shoot—fright. (As Holly Golightly said in the novella: "I knew damn well I'd never be a movie star. It's too hard; and if you're intelligent, it's too embarrassing.") But, in 1955, she told an interviewer for *Cosmopolitan* that "I've often been depressed and deeply disappointed in myself. You can even say that I hated myself at certain periods." Later, while on the set of *Charade* (1963), just a year after *Breakfast at Tiffany's* came out, Cary Grant told Hepburn that she had to learn to like herself a little more. "I've often thought about that," she said later in an interview. Her stream of movie successes in the mid-1950s, that included *Funny Face* (1957) and *Love in the Afternoon*, were punctuated with bouts of exhaustion.

"That was my mother's world: feelings and emotions," her son, Sean Hepburn Ferrer, would say. "Yet, her emotions were never quite peaceful . . . She was truly scared on some level. She was basically a very insecure person," he said, "whose very insecurity made everyone fall in love with her." Sean was born from Hepburn's marriage to Mel Ferrer, the actor/director/producer twelve years her senior, whom she met in 1953, but the couple had earlier suffered tremendous grief when her first two pregnancies ended in miscarriage. As she told her son later, "That was the closest I came to feeling that I was going to lose my mind."

As the 1950s drew toward their close, Hepburn was, in the opinion of biographer Donald Spoto, "aware that roles for her were becoming alarmingly repetitive . . . a certain stasis had affected both her range and her appeal." But in 1958, only two years before the first approach for *Breakfast at Tiffany's*, she made *The Nun's Story* (1959); the role of Sister Luke,

and the people she met researching the part had, she said, a profoundly enriching effect on her. She wrote a letter to director Fred Zinnemann to discuss her thoughts about the screenplay and her roles: "I am bothered by the fact that Sister Luke calls herself a 'failure' at the end of our story. She is too intelligent to display what sounds to me like a false humility. I still wish she could somehow express herself as having failed as a nun, but that her hopes and faith have been reborn at the thought of being able to function as a free human being . . ." Her judgment prevailed and script changes were made.

The twelve months that followed would be among the most packed in any life. A few years before, Ferrer had lead Hepburn into King Vidor's *War and Peace* (1956)—not, perhaps, her most successful role. Now, in the summer of 1958, hard from the shoot of *The Nun's Story*, he lead her into making his strange *Green Mansions* (1959), as a wild child found in the South American jungle. From there, she was rushed into another even less likely (and less successful) project, John Huston's *The Unforgiven* (1960), this despite the fact that she was once again pregnant. The longed-for pregnancy survived a serious riding accident, in which she crushed several vertebrae, but in May 1959, the baby was stillborn. Hepburn was seriously depressed, smoking three packs of cigarettes a day, weighing just eighty pounds and with her nails bitten to the quick.

In July of that year she traveled to Europe for a premiere of *The Nun's Story*, and met her father for the first time in years in Dublin. But in keeping with the family tradition of restraint in which Hepburn had been raised, the reunion passed off without tears, and in "polite pleasantries," her son says. "Knowing my mother, I don't think she ever had 'that good cry' about it. She saved it. Unknowingly, maybe she saved it for those moments on the screen."

The doctors prescribed a break from work, and she rallied. From Dublin she went to Paris, where she did

an enjoyable shoot with the great fashion photographer Richard Avedon—an old acquaintance, and the model for Fred Astaire's photographer in *Funny Face*—for *Harper's Bazaar*. By the end of the year, she was pregnant again. Determined to protect this pregnancy, she retreated to the home she and Ferrer had bought in Switzerland, on a hill overlooking Lake Lucerne. While plans for *Breakfast at Tiffany's* were getting underway in the United States, she was living there, quietly. Her son Sean was born in Lucerne on July 17, 1960. The joy, she said, was impossible to describe, and all the more so for the traumas that had come before it.

As she told broadcaster Larry King, "The one thing I dreamed of in my life was to have children of my own. It always boils down to the same thing. Not only receiving love, but wanting desperately to give it . . . almost needing to give it." Are there echoes here of Holly Golightly? Not the Holly who, in Capote's book, loses a baby and hardly allows herself to care, but the Holly determined to provide for her brother Fred by whatever means necessary?

PREVIOUS PAGE: Her role in The Nun's Story *had a special resonance for Hepburn. BELOW AND OVERLEAF RIGHT: The birth of Sean just a few weeks before* Breakfast at Tiffany's *gave Hepburn a depth of emotion she used for the movie.*

"My acting must come from inside—there is no other place it could come from. I can't fall back on technique," Hepburn said once. There is little doubt that the actress's experiences colored Holly's character, who at last surrenders so movingly to love. Hepburn came to *Breakfast at Tiffany's* fresh from an absolute roller coaster of emotions and life experiences. No wonder she was of a divided mind when they approached her to do the movie. She was reluctant to go to America and shoot through the autumn, but her husband urged her to do the project, and she had a child to provide for now.

To Alexander Walker, the respected London movie critic, "Holly Golightly's search for happiness coincided with Hepburn's re-evaluation of what life held for her." Holly hadn't found what she wanted and was filling the gap with lovers, just as Hepburn, he suggested, had been filling in with movies until the first of her two children came along. It isn't an idea to appeal to her fans, but bearing a child was, by her own testimony, more crucial than movies to her sense of identity.

As she told a reporter from London's *Daily Mail* years later, "I wanted lots of babies. That's been a theme in my life . . . from the time I had Sean, I hung onto my marriage because of him, and more and more, I began to resent the time I spent away from him on location. That was always the real me. The movies were fairy tales." Decades later, companion Robert Wolders would say, "Marilyn Monroe would probably have been allowed to play the character as created in the book, but they, unfortunately, wouldn't allow Hepburn to do that. I've found myself wishing she could have done the part as written. People didn't know how earthy and how true to life Audrey could be." Hepburn said herself, "I always wondered if I risked enough on that one. I should have been a little more outrageous. But at the time, as a new mother, I was about as wild as I could be."

OPPOSITE: *Hepburn once said that the love of an animal was the purest emotion anyone could experience.*

CHAPTER FOUR
THE CAST

In the end, it was agent Kurt Frings who found the word to make Holly Golightly's morality acceptable. He described her as a "kook," rather than a call girl, and Hepburn agreed. "That sounds better," she said. "Kook" was one of the buzzwords of the early 1960s—a vulnerable free spirit for whom innocence, rather than experience, was the main protection against the world. As noted by Paramount: "Our own Holly Golightly, as created first by Truman Capote, is a 'kookie' synthesis of all those lovely playgirls you find, or hope to find, in the cities. The part is, to offer the understatement of the decade, a departure for Miss Hepburn, whose roles up to now have not embraced 'kookiness.'" While the movie was still shooting, the unit publicist, a veteran showbiz writer named Cameron Shipp, had already put out a press release on the subject:

> "'Kook' is a word frequently employed by the offspring of this bewildered generation.
>
> 'She's a "kook," and all that jazz,' they say. But what do they mean, dad?
>
> Kook is not, as everybody associated with *Breakfast at Tiffany's* knows, a beatnik term. Couldn't be. The star is Audrey Hepburn, not Tawdry Hepburn.
>
> 'A kook is Zsa Zsa Gabor in the kitchen,' says Hepburn's co-star, George Peppard. (He's the kook-star.)
>
> 'Or,' George adds, 'a kook is a girl who puts Scotch in the coffee.'
>
> 'A kook is a kick with a coo,' says Buddy Ebsen, who plays a horse doctor in the picture.
>
> 'A kook is a skirt with a kick,' says Patricia Neal.
>
> 'A kook is a kitten who'll never grow up to be cat,' says producer Martin Jurow.
>
> 'A kook is a cute snook with a look,' says Betty Abbott, the famous script girl.
>
> 'I'm the kook and the kookie isn't grumbling,' says Audrey Hepburn.
>
> Send your definitions to the editor. Inclose box tops. Kookie box tops, of course."

Perhaps the very stressing of the word shows the level of anxiety the character of Holly Golightly still aroused. George Axelrod, after all, had faced several different challenges in converting Capote's novella for the big screen. The first involved plot. Capote's was not, as Axelrod told *Show* magazine when the movie came out, "really a story for the pictures." He goes on to explain: "Nothing really happened in the book. All we had was this glorious girl—a perfect part for Hepburn. We didn't want to do an *Auntie Mame* or *I Am a Camera* all over again, and, yet, we had the same problem here: no hero. Just a neuter, uninvolved narrator. What we had to do was devise a story, get a central romantic relationship . . ."

"Axelrod followed the novel, but he added a plot, a love story, for commercial reasons. I don't mean for money, but for audience approval," said Blake Edwards at the time. Paramount's original 1961 trailer set out the agenda clearly: "Audrey Hepburn and George Peppard searching for love in the big town but sharing only part of their lives—until they find the moment of deep, warm truth that can't be hidden, even by the oddball antics on the brittle surface of New York."

But, perhaps, this was not just a question of sending the audience home happy. At the end of the movie, Holly's renunciation of her plans to fly off to Brazil in search of love and of her proclaimed independence, represent a kind of atonement for the freedom of her sexuality. If the moral that might be drawn sounds rather anti-liberation, that probably seemed like a good thing to viewers scarce out of the 1950s.

The issue of Holly's profession did not go away. To modern audiences, the cheerfully cynical manipulation of, say, a Marilyn Monroe in *Gentlemen Prefer Blondes* back in 1953 looks far more daring than anything on offer by the end of the decade—but in that film, the goal of Monroe's character was marriage. In *Breakfast at Tiffany's*, by contrast, Holly's

profession was meant to raise some eyebrows—even that scene when she crawls platonically into bed with Paul wasn't altogether safe. This is, after all, a girl who lives by getting men to give her fifty dollars "for the powder room." Does that make her a hooker? Maybe not in itself, but it's hard to reconcile with a 1950s' ideal of purity.

The Holly of Capote's novella was very frank: "Not that I've warmed the multitudes some people say. . . . I've only had eleven lovers—not counting anything that happened before I was thirteen because, after all, that just *doesn't* count. Eleven. Does that make me a whore?" At that time, the popular answer was probably yes.

Breakfast at Tiffany's would be a movie made on the cusp of the changing times. In the 1950s there were still morals clauses in Hollywood contracts. While the 1930s had seen great heroines, and the movies of the war years showed women dealing bravely with the crisis, the 1950s saw a lot of folksy movies—*Seven Brides for Seven Brothers* (1954)—and the tamed tomboys of *Annie Get Your Gun* (1950) and *Calamity Jane* (1953). *A Star is Born* (1954), with Judy Garland declaring that her great achievement is to be Mrs. Norman Maine, was another. Hollywood's preferred female characters of the 1950s (the girlish bobbysoxers apart) were the home-makers and the natural-born home-breakers: big-breasted blondes à la Marilyn Monroe and Jayne Mansfield.

PREVIOUS PAGES: *Contact sheets of publicity stills from the shoot.* OPPOSITE: *Holly before her first meeting with Paul.*

As the new decade dawned, the movie industry was taking tentative steps toward the sexual revolution. The Motion Picture Association of America would very soon be forced to rethink its censorship code. In 1960, Elizabeth Taylor played a self-destructive call girl/nymphomaniac in *Butterfield 8*; William Holden fell for a Chinese prostitute in *The World of Suzie Wong*; and Shirley MacLaine managed to play the part of a girl who slept with a number of men without losing the audience's sympathy in *The Apartment*. But *The Apartment* presented MacLaine as a married man's victim rather than villainess, the prostitute in *The World of Suzie Wong* was at once protected and marginalized by her exotic foreign status, and *Butterfield 8* was regarded as, frankly, risky.

The ice was beginning to break. In the early 1960's Helen Gurley Brown's *Sex and the Single Girl* advised, "You may marry or you may not. In today's world that is no longer the big question for women." And writing in the September, 1962 issue of *Esquire*, Gloria Steinem declared, "Writers in or out of Hollywood should be warned that they can no longer build plots on the loss of virginity or fainting pregnant heroines and expect to be believed." But even then, in 1962, when Richard Burton and Elizabeth Taylor fell in love on the set of *Cleopatra*, there was a suggestion in Congress they might be barred from the United States on the grounds of undesirability. In the same year, the president of Vassar College warned that any student wishing to indulge in premarital sex should withdraw from their studies; a mother pregnant with a thalidomide baby was refused an abortion by the courts; another was arrested for issuing birth control information to her teenage daughter.

What's more is that this was not a moment when Hollywood was eager to take risks of any description. The old-style "dream-factory" system was on the way out. Stars were no longer virtually indentured by exclusive contracts, and fewer pictures were coming to be shot on the studio home ground with more acquired from outside. Studios were mounting a big-budget, 3-D, CinemaScope rear-guard action against the encroachments of television. Nonetheless, by 1959, the total studio output was less than half that of 1950. The industry itself was struggling, and in a mood to regard the presentiments of change ahead as a threat, rather than an opportunity.

So it might seem perverse that in one specific way George Axelrod's screenplay actually upped the sexual tension from Capote's story by inventing "2-E" (so-called because of her initials, E. E. for Emily Eustace), the wealthy older woman keeping the young male writer. It's a decision hard to understand today, when Holly's sexual freedom seems the norm, and we find it quite easy to swallow the implication that, with few other options in her life, she sleeps with men for money. But to find a young man doing it—and a young man with other talents, at that—does still arouse a degree of prejudice.

George Axelrod's rationale is interesting. Having made Capote's character of the passive writer ("the hero," as Axelrod calls him) into "a red-blooded heterosexual, we still had to keep him apart, or the audiences would wonder why they didn't just get together and pow. Our solution was to make them both busy being kept by other people. So then when you get the one bed scene in the picture, he's just too tired to do anything."

Perhaps the device was also a way to keep some of the loucheness of Capote's novella without allowing it to compromise Hepburn's trademark purity. That aura was so powerful, Blake Edwards says, that he suspects by the end of the movie most viewers still

OPPOSITE: *Peppard's blend of innocence and strength was what the producers wanted for the role of Paul.*

PAUL

Okay, run away! But pretty soon there won't be any place
left for you to run to. Then you're going to have to stop
and figure out what it is you're actually running from.

HOLLY

Let go of the door! I'll miss my plane!

PAUL

You've been running all of your life...don't you see the
pattern…listen to what I'm saying...it'll give
you something to think about while you're flying over
the jungle in your silver plane...Your whole life's
been spent running and hiding...you're too smart a girl to
go on kidding yourself! **A ranch in Mexico with Fred?
Rusty Trawler? The Queen of the Pampas?** All crap you
dreamed up to protect you from the thing you're really
scared of.

HOLLY

Which is?

PAUL

Men...or **a** man rather...

HOLLY

Are you crazy? I've had fifteen different...

PAUL

Don't brag. It's eleven. You told me so yourself. And
that's the whole point. Eleven instead of one. Why?
Because you're **afraid**! Afraid if you ever let yourself
love one man...one man who was **possible**...who
could love you back ...

HOLLY

Shut up!

PAUL

You know I'm right...as long as I played the game
with you...as long as you and I were parallel lines...
everything was fine. Then one day those parallel
lines **met**. And you were so scared you couldn't stand it...
I love you, Holly, and there's nothing to be scared of...

haven't really put two and two together to grasp what Holly does for a living. But Axelrod's invention serves another function, too. One of the weaknesses of Sumner Locke Elliott's treatment had arguably been that his writer had held too much of the moral high ground, and in a priggish rather than a sympathetic way. Admirable, maybe; likeable, never—and not, therefore, a character with whom Holly was ever really likely to wind up with.

The character Peppard plays, on the other hand, was, indeed, to be the rescuer, the one whose moral, or at least emotional, compass points the way. But he, too, first had to have made a journey—to have been, as a speech in Axelrod's first script draft put it, on "parallel lines" with Holly. In that first draft, Paul's speech comes near the end of the movie, after Holly has pushed the cat out of the taxi, and told the cabbie to drive away (see the script on the opposite page).

That dialogue had disappeared by the final draft of the movie, but it represents an aspect of Paul's character that continued to be important, although it was one with which the actor's own vision of the role would not always agree.

★ ★ ★ ★ ★ ★ ★

While Hepburn's importance to *Breakfast at Tiffany's* is undisputable, opinions are more mixed as to Peppard's suitability, and some of the doubts come from the very heart of the production story. Edwards had originally wanted Steve McQueen in the role, and still admits to uncertainty about Peppard. They personally liked each other, he insists, but if he were pressed as to whether he'd cast him today, he says, "I doubt if I would. He just didn't have—whatever it was I wanted. He wasn't my cup of tea." But the casting director praised Peppard's "strong physical presence;" the script described the character as "dark, tough, sensitive, and handsome." (And "about twenty minutes away from being *badly* in need of a shave.")

LEFT: *Peppard in an off-duty moment.*

In 1960—just three years after a supporting role in *The Strange One* gave him his first break and released him from a life of driving taxis and working on construction sites—Peppard's career had already taken off in such a way that the Paramount press claimed he was "regarded as the hottest young actor in Hollywood, a comer with the impact of Jimmy Dean or a young Clark Gable." But *Breakfast at Tiffany's* was to be his big break. "In many ways," says producer Richard Shepherd, it was "the most important leading role that he ever had." Patricia Neal, who played opposite him as 2-E, remembered doing a scene with him at the Actors Studio, in New York City, before either of them were cast in *Breakfast at Tiffany's*: "A new young actor who had just made his Broadway debut. George Peppard was handsome and sexy—my happily pregnant state made me particularly sensitive to his boyish charm and energy." Neal herself believed in the deep analysis of the Method school of acting, but Peppard's belief in the Method went much deeper. Perhaps Peppard's adherence to the Method was part and parcel of the problems on the set of *Breakfast at Tiffany's*.

Breakfast at Tiffany's really was the movie that almost didn't happen: not only did Capote not want Hepburn, and Edwards not want George Peppard, Edwards himself was the second name scheduled for the director's chair. John Frankenheimer—then known chiefly as a young documentarian and TV director, though he'd go on to make *Birdman of Alcatraz* and *The Manchurian Candidate* (both 1962)—had been the name originally attached, and trumpeted as "long considered television's most outstanding director" in an early Paramount press release. But in the end, Frankenheimer was dropped because the producers feared his style was "too dark" for what they wanted to do. (Axelrod, who made *The Manchurian Candidate* with Frankenheimer, later said that the change to the "more experienced" Edwards was down to Hepburn, who had director approval.) Edwards, then in his late thirties, was also best known

for his television work, especially for the successful series *Peter Gunn* and *Mr. Lucky*, but the producers had been impressed by the "spirited pace" with which he had directed the comedy *Operation Petticoat*. But *Breakfast at Tiffany's* would still be his great opportunity. "I'd have done it if I had to crawl all the way up the Walk of Fame," Edwards says frankly.

Axelrod, some stories said, bickered with Edwards on set, and certainly in the transition to film, the sexual tensions of his script were taken down a degree. Luckily, the secondary roles fell into place more easily. It was Richard Shepherd's wife, Judy, who suggested Patricia Neal for the role of 2-E. "We wanted someone with no nonsense and she could play that strong, subterranean sexual role," Shepherd says. "Someone who had strength and could be domineering, elegant in a bossy kind of way."

"I sort of understood the character I played," Patricia Neal says now. "I guess I didn't get 'it' from my husband, and I 'had' to have a man." She was asked to dye her dark hair red, so as not to distract from Hepburn. Her family approved the idea of a "flaming red, carrot-topped" mother, so she agreed. Neal was married to Roald Dahl, the noted author of children's books. Her third baby had just been born, less than two weeks after Hepburn's son, and in her early thirties, she had already begun to feel Hollywood had forgotten her. Here, however, she would be required to play the very antithesis of a family woman: a "very stylish girl," prepared to alienate the audience's sympathy at every turn.

The role of Holly's husband Doc was a subtle one, but casting Buddy Ebsen was an easy choice. "Buddy is Buddy. An old vaudeville hoofer. It was a brilliant bit of casting," Edwards says. Ebsen, who had started out as a dancing double act with his sister Vilma, had already run the gamut of Broadway, cabaret, and naval service in the war. In the 1930s he'd danced with Shirley Temple in *Captain January*

(1936), and with Judy Garland in *Broadway Melody of 1938*. He was due to star with Judy Garland again when fate intervened and chose him for one of the great showbiz hard-luck stories.

Originally cast to play the Scarecrow in *The Wizard of Oz* (1939), Ebsen good-naturedly agreed to swap roles with Ray Bolger as the Tin Man, only to find himself fighting for breath in an oxygen tent after the aluminium dust with which he was coated spread through his skin to his lungs. He was out of the movie, his health (and his relationship with the Hollywood studios) permanently impaired. Meanwhile, the dangerous silver dust was hastily switched for a less volatile paste to color his replacement.

Of the other roles, Martin Balsam, as the Hollywood agent O. J. Berman, was a well-known actor who already had *On the Waterfront* (1954) and *Psycho* (1960) under his belt. The part of Holly's Brazilian admirer, "a wildly handsome Latin with the look of a shy bullfighter," as the script described him, went to "Vilallonga"—or, to give him his full title, Jose Luis de Vilallonga, Marqués de Castellbell y Grande de España, a Spanish aristocrat whose long and colorful career ultimately comprised authorship of more than thirty books, and appearances in seventy or more mostly European films. A sometime political exile,

ABOVE: *Patricia Neal took on a hard-edged elegance as the wealthy "other woman," 2-E.*

breeder of horses in Argentina, and later director of the Spanish edition of *Playboy* (besides himself often appearing in the gossip columns), Vilallonga had been recommended by Hepburn and Ferrer, who had met him in Paris; but this was also one of those pieces of secondary casting beloved of Edwards, where the performer brought a baggage-load of useful experience to the role.

Mickey Rooney, Edwards's old friend, was recruited to play the comic role of Holly's Japanese neighbor, Mr. Yunioshi. This was, as everyone involved now agrees, an inappropriate piece of casting that would cause trouble later down the line, but at the time no-one examined it too closely.

One of Cameron Shipp's press releases proclaimed that Edwards "wants to meet every high-fashion model in New York who's six feet tall or over. Girl must be gorgeous, svelte, photogenic—and absolutely a timbertopper." In the end, the role of the statuesque Mag Wildwood went to the five-foot-eleven-inch Dorothy Whitney, stepdaughter of Raymond Massey

and stepsister to actress Anna and actor Daniel. There was still one outstanding bit of casting that needed to be done. That of "the big tom," who has a "thug face," and "yellowish pointy eyes," as described by Capote. As Shipp explains:

> "'Putney,' a twelve-pound tomcat with no previous dramatic experience, arrived in Hollywood yesterday from New York to start training for a part.
>
> Since cats seldom perform more than one trick at a time, more than a dozen cats are actually being used in *Breakfast at Tiffany's*. All are identical. But Putney gets billing as Audrey Hepburn's pet. He is called 'Cat.'
>
> 'He'll be a good actor,' [trainer] Frank Inn said. 'He's a real New York-type cat, just what we want. In no time at all I'm going to make a Method, or Lee Strasberg-type, cat out of him.'"

ABOVE: Mickey Rooney pictured in 1949 (left) and, controversially, as Mr Yunioshi (right). OPPOSITE: Cat is a regular spectator to the drama of Holly's life.

The studio publicity proved to be more concerned with the cheerful generation of a stream of good stories than with accuracy. It was later declared that the principal cat (stunt doubles apart) was Orangey, rather than Putney, a veteran who had already played the title role in *Rhubarb* (1951) years before. But the striking thing was the public's appetite for any information, no matter how trivial, relating to the film.

In July 1960, with shooting scheduled to start in October, Capote wrote to Hepburn, congratulating her on the birth of her new baby and making a gracious capitulation over the casting: "I have no opinion of the movie script, never having had the opportunity to read it. But since Hepburn and Holly are both such wonderful girls, I feel nothing can defeat either of them."

One final hurdle had to be overcome. The final screenplay had been sent to the all-powerful Motion Picture Association, the moral watchdog of the movie industry, whose Production Code would be used to decide whether the irregularities of Holly and her profession (and, now, Paul and his) had been sufficiently smoothed away. August saw a flurry of correspondence. The MPA's verdict declared: "This basic story seems to be acceptable under the requirements of the Production Code," but "it contains certain elements which should be corrected if we are to be able to approve the finished picture." Among the causes for the MPA's concern were "the several undressing scenes involving Holly . . . these would have to be handled with extreme care to avoid any attempt to exploit any partial or seminudity." Moreover, "the relationship between 2-E and Paul as presently described in this script is unacceptably blunt. In this regard, we call your attention to the following unacceptable details:

> ". . . she has very gently
> begun to unbutton his shirt."

> ". . . pushes him away from her
> and toward the bed."

And so on. The "numerous uses of profanity in this present script" should be eliminated, "except for one or two uses of the word, 'hell,' which you feel absolutely indispensable." And, most important of all, after the day out, when the relationship between Paul and Holly comes to a head:

> "It was agreed that there would be
> no indication of a sex affair between Holly
> and Paul. It was agreed that her line, 'I just
> thought of something that neither of us has
> ever done. At least not together,' if retained
> at all, will not in any way refer to the sex
> affair, and this scene will be played outside
> the house and not inside Paul's apartment
> as presently indicated. You understand,
> of course, that our final judgment will
> be based on the finished picture."

While a sour ending to their letter, it was, nonetheless, a basic go-ahead.

Breakfast at Tiffany's was underway.

PREVIOUS PAGE: *The scene where Holly innocently clambers into Paul's bed was, at the time, considered risqué.* OPPOSITE: *Hepburn's ice blue coat was replaced by the burnt orange version in the final shoot.* OVERLEAF: *A letter from the Motion Picture Association discussing the cuts needed before* Breakfast at Tiffany's *would meet the moral standard of the day.*

August 17, 1960

Mr. Luigi Luraschi
Paramount Pictures Corporation
5451 Marathon Street
Hollywood 38, California

Dear Mr. Luraschi:

This letter goes to you in confirmation of the
discussion held at your office recently with Messrs.Jurow
and Shepherd concerning the screenplay for your proposed
production, BREAKFAST AT TIFFANY'S.

As we told you at that time, while this basic story
seems to be acceptable under the requirements of the Production Code, it contains certain elements which should be
corrected if we are to be able to approve the finished
picture.

You will recall it was agreed that Holly would explain that her marriage to Doc had "never been a real marriage at all, and that when she left him, the marriage had
been annulled".

Also, we discussed the several undressing scenes
involving Holly, and agreed that these would have to be
handled with extreme care to avoid any attempt to exploit
any partial or semi-nudity.

Page 15: Holly should be wearing a full slip rather
than a half-slip and brassiere.

Page 24 et seq.: The relationship between 2E and
Paul as presently described in this script is unacceptably
blunt. In this regard, we call your attention to the following unacceptable details:

> "...she has very gently begun to unbutton
> his shirt."

> "...pushes him away from her and toward
> the bed."

"Paul is asleep on the bed...he is smiling
benignly in his sleep."

"Her features take on the same benign smile."

"2E, dressed for the street, is coming out
of the bathroom. She moves about the room,
straightening up. Emptying ashtrays and
clearing away glasses."

"2E, her domestic chores finished, goes
to the bed and lovingly pulls the covers up
around the sleeping Paul. She kisses him
very gently. He does not awaken. She
starts to go - then - almost as an after-
thought - opens her purse and takes out
three hundred dollars in fifty dollar bills
which she places the desk. She kisses Paul
once more and tiptoes out, closing the door
softly behind her."

Page 28: Please eliminate Holly's line, "Three
hundred? She's very generous...Is that by the hour?"

Page 28: Also, please eliminate Holly's line, "I
was just trying to let you know I understand. Not only
that, I approve."

Page 29: Please eliminate Holly's line, "You must
be absolutely exhausted..."

Page 72: As we agreed, the striptease dancer would
not be shown.

Page 96: It was agreed that there will be no indi-
cation of a sex affair between Holly and Paul. It was
agreed that her line, "I just thought of something that
neither of us has ever done. At least not together...",
if retained at all, will not in any way refer to the sex
affair, and this scene will be played outside the house
and not inside Paul's apartment as presently indicated.

You will recall that we discussed the numerous uses
of profanity in this present script, and agreed that all
would be eliminated except one or two uses of the word,
"hell", which you feel absolutely indispensable.

Edith Head

CHAPTER FIVE
THE STYLE

"It was a warm evening, nearly summer, and she wore a slim cool black dress, black sandals, a pearl choker. For all her chic thinness, she had an almost breakfast-cereal air of health, a soap and lemon cleanness, a rough pink darkening in the cheeks. Her mouth was large, her nose upturned. A pair of dark glasses blotted out her eyes. It was a face beyond childhood, yet this side of belonging to a woman. I thought her anywhere between sixteen and thirty; as it turned out, she was two months shy of her nineteenth birthday."

—Truman Capote, *Breakfast at Tiffany's*

When Hepburn made *Breakfast at Tiffany's*, she was thirty-one, not eighteen, and already a style icon. But it is the look of this movie—the look she and Hubert de Givenchy perfected together—that most encapsulates what we think of as "Audrey style." The oversized sunglasses, the scarf trailing behind—and, of course, those layers of pearls that speak so clearly of Holly's longing for a larger life. After the movie came out, a copycat version of the orange coat she wore to visit Tiffany's with Paul was quickly in the stores, and "everyone wanted that mink hat," says Letitia Baldrige, Tiffany's then director of public relations and later Jackie Kennedy's chief of staff.

The movie's chosen styles were Hepburn's, too. Perhaps it's because the looks she wore on screen reflect her personality that they still strike a chord with women today. Hepburn's favorite private wardrobe throughout her life was jeans and a polo shirt or turtleneck sweater, the very thing Holly wears when she croons "Moon River." Hepburn's public costume was the work of her long-time friend and collaborator, Hubert de Givenchy. "His are the only clothes in which I am myself. He is far more than a couturier, he is a creator of personality," Hepburn has said. "My magic was hers," said Givenchy, describing their sense of collaboration.

Hepburn's clear-cut personal style was an important part of the decade that ran from the mid-1950s to the mid-1960s. As Cecil Beaton wrote in *Vogue*, in November 1954, "No one can doubt that Hepburn's appearance succeeds because it embodies the spirit of today . . . the striking personality that embodies our new Zeitgeist." Director Michael Powell, meeting her around the same time, said more simply, "She was the right shape for that year." Though the "Audrey look" seems close to perfect now, it was something of a challenge when she first appeared on the scene.

Edith Head, the legendary Paramount production designer, credited with overall control for the costumes on *Breakfast at Tiffany's*, met Hepburn in 1952, and later wrote up the young actress's perceptive eye and fashion expertize in rosy colors, saying, "I knew she would be the perfect mannequin for anything I would make. I knew it would be a great temptation to design clothes that would overpower her. I could have used her to show off my talents and detract from hers, but I didn't. I considered doing it, believe me."

Head and Hepburn had worked together to create her look as the incognito princess in *Roman Holiday*: the bobbysoxer uniform of flared skirt, socks over stockings, and flat shoes. But it was Hepburn herself who suggested the grace note of the broad belt. Soon, everyone was wearing one. When *Sabrina* came along a year later, Head turned up with her designs only to learn that Hepburn, for this role of the American chauffeur's daughter who reinvents herself in Paris, had persuaded Paramount to let her buy some of her clothes in the real Paris ateliers. The Hollywood-oriented Head, it was thought, might not understand the style of European glamour needed for Sabrina's Parisian transformation and triumphant return to Long Island. It was then that Hepburn first met Givenchy.

PREVIOUS PAGE AND ABOVE: *Though Givenchy created Hepburn's most famous dresses, Edith Head had overall responsibility for the costume design. Not all the outfits illustrated in her sketches—above—made it into the finished film.* OPPOSITE: *Hepburn and Givenchy walking by the Seine in Paris, 1982.*

She was already an admirer of the twenty-six-year-old couturier, who had not long before left Schiaparelli to found his own house. He, by contrast, had never heard of her. When told that Miss Hepburn, the movie star, was coming to visit him, he imagined clothing the star of *Bringing Up Baby* and *The Philadelphia Story* (1940)—Katharine Hepburn, not Audrey Hepburn. Almost instantly, however, he realized his good fortune, that here was a woman who embodied his own creed, who shared his sensibility. Givenchy—an aristocrat, like Hepburn, a European Protestant, and an adventurous spirit raised in an austere school—made no compromise for a woman's figure. With Hepburn, none was needed—he chose to accentuate the height and thinness Hollywood might have considered her flaws.

Givenchy described his studio as a laboratory, not without reason. It was he who, in 1957, popularized the sack dress, precursor of the fashion revolution credited to the 1960s; he was also one of the first designers to accept that a hemline could go above the knee. Is it fanciful to suggest that, alongside his huge kindness to Hepburn, she found—and welcomed—in him something of the demanding quality she would have found in the maestros of the ballet?

Nothing could be more feminine (in a restrained way) than a Givenchy dress—think of the floral number in *Funny Face*. Yet Hepburn spoke of his dresses as armor. "Clothes, as they say, make the man, but they certainly have, with me, given me the confidence I often needed," she reflected. She was, perhaps, someone who felt most at ease when under authority.

Givenchy's clothes would give her a cosmopolitan sophistication. Her fame would give him, the man who banned press from his shows, publicity and accessibility—after all, the minimalist elegance they developed together at least looked easy to copy. "My look is attainable," said Hepburn herself.

ABOVE: *The dress shirt in which Holly first encounters Paul.*
OPPOSITE: *Perhaps the slightly uncharacteristic outfit she wears for an evening with Jose reflects the inherent problems of that relationship.*

TIFFANY

and Pauline Trigère, a forty-eight-year-old French-born émigré, famed for her tailoring, as designer of the clothes for Patricia Neal as 2-E. Paramount described 2-E's wardrobe as "smart, chic, simple, and outrageously expensive"—very "New York," in other words. Paramount put out a press release about George Peppard's wardrobe:

> "George Peppard . . . gets a stylish break in this picture—upward of $4,000 worth of free tailoring. Ordinarily, actors [as opposed to actresses] supply their own clothes for all pictures, but Peppard's many changes, from tweeds to white tie, are manifold and far beyond the call of dramatic duty.
>
> Peppard has been undergoing fittings for several weeks, but not as gratefully as you might think.
>
> 'Standing still for fittings while three tailors play you like a grand piano is the hardest work I've ever done,' he says. 'A horse shouldn't work so hard, even a clothes horse, which I am, decidedly, not.'"

Hair was done by Nellie Manley, who had already worked with Hepburn on *Funny Face*, and make-up was by Wally Westmore, scion of the famous Hollywood make-up family, who had worked not only on that picture, but also on *Sabrina* and *Roman Holiday*. But Givenchy is the name people remember from this movie. The designer flew from Paris to Switzerland several times for consultation with Hepburn, then Mel Ferrer flew to Paris, saw the Givenchy collection, and took his selection back to Hepburn. The entire wardrobe was then brought to Hollywood, and then to New York, as publicist

"Women can look like Audrey Hepburn by flipping out their hair, buying the large sunglasses and the little sleeveless dresses." Perhaps part of Holly Golightly's appeal, as she flings on garments for her visit to Sing Sing, is that she makes it look so easy. Some of Hepburn's most notable roles, from *Sabrina* to *Funny Face* to *My Fair Lady*, rely on our perennial fascination with the Cinderella-like magic of the transformation scene, that moment when the plain girl becomes the chic woman.

It is Edith Head's name that leads the official credits for the costumes of *Breakfast at Tiffany's*, followed by Givenchy's as designer of Hepburn's wardrobe

ABOVE: Publicity shot capitalizing on the lure of the Tiffany jewels. OPPOSITE: Hepburn and Neal relaxing between takes.

SS99

THE LITTLE BLACK DRESS

"Scheherazade is easy. A little black dress is difficult," said Coco Chanel—and she, of all other fashion designers, is the one who should know. It was Chanel who, in 1926, presented a long-sleeved black crepe dress which *Vogue* likened to the model T Ford. It would become "a uniform for all women of taste," the magazine wrote, prophetically.

Chanel was reflecting the new spirit of freedom and activity enjoyed by women in the years after the First World War. "I make clothes women can live in, breathe in, feel comfortable in and look young in," she said. So ubiquitous has the Little Black Dress become in the decades since that it is hard to realize now just how startling was the idea of putting fashionable women into a color and a plain fabric traditionally worn only by widows and maidservants—how startling the idea that true elegance might lie in a garment so simple (and so capable of carrying a busy woman right through from day to night) that anyone might wear it. Historically the color of death (and of power—because to produce black fabric took such a quantity of expensive dye), black had become the color of servants and of the mourning, the unhappy. And, everyday wear though black has now become, it still carries a faint element of the forbidden, the dangerous. Perhaps that is one reason it appeals to Holly Golightly.

Capote suggested one reason why black would work for Holly when he wrote in the novella of his vivid heroine's taste for the plain colors that made "her, herself, shine so." Another would be the sheer practicality of a Little Black Dress—every good-time girl of Holly's day, with many engagements and not much money, knew the value of a black dress, which could be dressed up with a whole variety of accessories, and wouldn't need to be cleaned too frequently. But it is also a garment that can send a variety of messages, and perhaps there is something there that speaks to Holly's ambiguity.

Every generation since Chanel's has found their own way of wearing black, from the intellectuals of the Left Bank to the Goths of London and the working women of the early Eighties. The Little Black Dress itself has shown almost as much versatility. It can be the ultimate non-statement, if that is what you want, but it can also be the garment that speaks most clearly. When Elizabeth Hurley wore Versace's kilt-pinned Little Black Dress, it positively shrieked "look at me!" When Diana, Princess of Wales, broke with royal protocol to wear a brief black dress on the evening her estranged husband was making his televized bid for popularity, it said that she now considered herself liberated from the royal family. Every designer has created a Little Black Dress, from Balenciaga to Claire McCardell, Armani to Lagerfeld, and perhaps *Breakfast at Tiffany's* played a part in fostering that popularity. As *Vogue* put it 1944: "Ten out of ten women have one—but ten out of ten want another because a little black dress leads the best-rounded life. Is a complete chameleon about moods and times and places. Has the highest potential chic (only if well-handled). Has the longest open season." Holly Golightly would agree. In 1951 *Woman and Beauty* told its readers: "Invest your all in one good little black dress." The advice hasn't changed today.

Cameron Shipp was pleased to announce: "A truck load of luggage—thirty-six large pieces—was unloaded from the plane when Hepburn returned to Hollywood to start her new Jurow-Shepherd picture, *Breakfast at Tiffany's*."

While *Breakfast at Tiffany's* was shooting, Hepburn was the first elected to the Fashion Hall of Fame. In the Paramount press notes, Hepburn described her favorite outfits: "a huge black straw hat, just the thing for visiting Sing Sing," another hat that has "a blob of feathers," a cocktail dress, "very sassy looking and wonderfully humorous when one walks . . . a good dress for 21" . . . and a softly feminine dress "on the edge of being a little outrageous."

But one outfit is particularly associated with Hepburn, and with Holly: the Little Black Dress.

Part of the appeal of the Little Black Dress is that it can be endlessly adapted to suit mood, season, or just time of day, and Holly rings the changes with expert versatility. She adds a hat, a pair of sunglasses, or chooses from a whole selection of earrings—the inventive use of accessories is the film's *other* great fashion story.

But there was a particular point to the elegance and, you might almost say, austerity of Hepburn's dressing to play the morally ambiguous Holly. "I always looked like such a good little girl," Hepburn has said, "and I always used that image to my advantage."

Capote had written of Holly in his novella that "there was a consequential good taste in the plainness of her clothes, the blues and gray and lack of luster that made her, herself, shine so." By the same token, Hepburn's son Sean has suggested that the Little Black Dress was nothing more nor less than "a magnifying glass to the soul"—a convincing explanation both of why it so suited Hepburn and why it remains a garment of safety and aspiration today.

ABOVE: (Top) Edith Head's sketches for yet another version of the Little Black Dress, and (below) for the casual trousers and sweater in which Holly croons Moon River. OVERLEAF: Hepburn and Blake Edwards confer, amid the bustle of the location shoot.

CHAPTER SIX
THE PLACE AND PEOPLE

New York City was as much a player in the love story with Hepburn as was George Peppard. In the original trailer, Paramount played up the mystique of the city, as the characters "breeze through the glitter and shimmer of New York as it has never been captured before." It is a city that never ceases to sizzle in the imagination. As Paramount press noted, "It all happens in NYC as of right now."

The years following World War II saw New York City attain new heights, both figuratively and literally. The European capitals were still suffering from the battering they had taken; the new glamour of the American Sunbelt cities lay ahead. In 1953, the writer Cyril Connolly declared, "If Paris is the setting for romance, New York is the perfect city in which to get over one, to get over anything. Here the lost *douceur de vivre* is forgotten and the intoxication of living takes its place."

But by 1960 there was another new spirit in the air. The age of Pop Art and Andy Warhol, of louche parties and loft living, was on the way, even while traces of the older style of glamour lingered. Norman Mailer had written of Capote's novella and its wartime setting, saying, "If you want to capture a period in New York, no other book has done it so well." The movie had a lot to live up to.

Capote once said, "New York is like a city made out of modeling clay. You can make it whatever you want." In a 1961 piece written for *Mademoiselle* magazine, Joan Didion declared that New York was the place for people to make *themselves* what they wanted. "Girls who come to New York are, above all, uncommitted. They seem to be girls who want to prolong the period when they can experiment, mess around, make mistakes . . . New York is full of people on this kind of leave of absence, of people with a feeling for the tangential adventure, the risk adventure, the interlude that's not likely to end in any double-ring ceremony." Holly Golightly helped make this sentiment a possibility.

For a movie so associated with New York City, it's surprising how little of *Breakfast at Tiffany's* was actually shot in the city. Eight days of location shooting took the film crew to the Central Promenade in Central Park, the exterior of the Women's Prison of Detention on Tenth Street, a brownstone house in the East Sixties, and the steps outside the New York Public Library. "And, of course, Tiffany's," wrote *New York Times* journalist Eugene Archer, "which opened its door to a movie company for the first time with forty guards and sales staff to keep an eye on the jewels."

At the time when almost everything was shot on a studio lot, it was considered noteworthy that the team was prepared to embark on location filming at all. Paramount issued a press release on the subject, quoting Blake Edwards: "We want to expose the cast

to the jangle, the roar, and the smell of New York. You watch what happens. A girl just naturally steps faster and brisker in New York."

In fact, before shooting started, the indefatigable Cameron Shipp put out another press release, quoting Martin Jurow on the decision to shoot in New York rather than "faster and cheaper" Los Angeles:

PAGE 96: *Peppard in Central Park, with the New York skyline behind him.* PREVIOUS PAGE: *This shot, cut from the final film, suggests the visual gag which allows Paul to mistake another girl for Holly.* OPPOSITE: *Neal and Peppard between shots.* ABOVE: *This all-encompassing shot was a ground-breaker at the time.*

"You get a dynamic response to the real thing. Flo Ziegfeld [the famous impresario] always dressed his showgirls in the best. They felt expensive, so they looked and acted expensive. So we'll expose our people to New York in the raw, rain, noise, tempo, and all. Audrey Hepburn and George Peppard have both played Broadway. They've been walking by our synthetic New York [on Paramount's lot] for weeks now, not noticing. But they'll come alive and tingle, when they get the real article."

But to our eyes, when the cast and crew moved to the Paramount lot, they would be going into an environment at least as exotic—more than sixty acres dedicated to the realistic creation of fantasy. The Paramount lot was impressive in scope, in the way that New York City is in authenticity. The lot boasts at least 150 buildings and employs roughly 2500 people on an average day. Rumor has it that there are miles of underground tunnels circling the lot, but no-one's actually dug it up to find out. Among the famous sights—the tank where Moses parted the Red Sea in *The Ten Commandments* (1956), the huge stage that has been used from the 1920s all the way up to the more recent *Star Trek* movies, fake sky for when L.A.'s cloudless blue is just too sunny—is the New York back lot, tucked into Paramount's Production Park. With its forty-six facades, and a top dressing of signs, props, and hoardings, the New York back lot can create the look and feel of six different blocks of New York City.

In 1983, a fire devastated the Paramount back lot, destroying the sets used in *The Godfather* (1972) and *Chinatown* (1974). Much of this surrogate "New York" was rebuilt, and is still in use. But the alley where the closing scenes of *Breakfast at Tiffany's* were shot was a permanent casualty.

For the duration of the New York shoot, many of the film crew and actors flew back and forth between the East Coast and Hollywood. Patricia Neal was not among them. She only had to walk around the corner from her own apartment to go to work on the Paramount lot. While Hepburn brought her little dog Famous, Patricia brought her husband Roald Dahl and their three small children (Olivia, Tessa, and baby Theo) "to watch her be a 'bad' woman."

Neal had been a girl from Tennessee, but she'd always dreamed of Broadway in New York City. In 1956, the Dahls rented an apartment across the street from Campbell's Funeral Chapel on Madison Avenue. The apartment above was owned by Clifford Odets and sublet by the young actress Valerie French; on the ninth floor, the Kandinsky sisters kept monkeys and cats. It is an environment that might have suited Holly Golightly.

Neal had only one scene with Hepburn, and found her to be "quite friendly." Indeed, in Hollywood, Hepburn invited Neal to her house for supper one night. "Mel [Ferrer] was very strict with her during production, so the evening was one drink, a light meal, and good night. I don't think the sun had even set by the time I got home. But I sure know how she kept her looks and figure." The Paramount press issued a release detailing Hepburn's sense of discipline: Hepburn "failed to see a single play during her visit [to New York]. She caught one performance of the Royal Ballet, then had a big night on the town—a visit to a soda fountain!"

OPPOSITE: Hepburn's terrier, Famous, was a regular visitor on set. OVERLEAF: Large crowds gathered to watch filming outside the New York Public Library.

ABOVE: *Rehearsing the scene where Holly sets off to Sing Sing.* OPPOSITE: *Peppard—alone in a crowd.*

But the working relationship of both women, and indeed of the director, with Peppard was less than happy. "George [Peppard] arrived on the set fully convinced of his star potential and felt that his character was the real center of attention," recollected Marty Jurow in his autobiography. "He was disappointed when Audrey didn't respond to him on a personal level and referred to her as 'The Happy Nun,'" a reference, presumably, to *The Nun's Story.* There was, moreover, a difference of working styles. Peppard was an analytical Method actor, looking into himself to find a greater realism for his role, while Hepburn worked on instinct, or on the kind of close instruction the great old directors with whom she'd often worked with were more than able to give. Echoes of this difference are evident in a press release put out by the studio in December.

Peppard, it said, "did the kissing seriously, and seemed to be putting his heart into it. But hear this," he complained, "my neck was craned in order to give Audrey's profile the best view. Audrey, who would possibly be the most exciting girl in the world to kiss if she were actually kissing—wasn't kissing. She was acting . . ."

"There was a difference between the way George Peppard worked on this movie and the way Hepburn—and even Patricia Neal—worked," Richard Shepherd says. "My memory is that she found his method was a little too intense. George was an intense young man. I don't think they were really close off-camera, and that might have had to do with the way George approached his part." On the other hand, Shepherd raves about Hepburn: "The most loving and giving woman to work with. I don't know another actress around who could play it the way Audrey played it. But Paramount had her under contract and the good Lord let us have her."

Neal, Peppard's old Actors Studio colleague, found a change had come over Peppard, who she had once found divine and "flirty." He had been spoiled, she said, looking back. "Blake Edwards was beautiful to work with, as was Audrey," Neal wrote in her autobiography, *As I Am.* "Only gorgeous George seemed to be chomping slightly at the bit. His character was written with a battered vulnerability that was totally appealing, but it did not correspond to George's image of a leading man. He seemed to want to be an old-time movie hunk." Later, she was, if anything, more fervent. "Boy, he'd gotten rotten. At the Actors Studio I'd adored him. But I loved the darling director."

She recalled that some of her lines were trimmed, presumably at Peppard's instigation, so she no longer appeared to dominate the scene in any way. Peppard and Blake "locked horns through most of the filming, almost coming to blows at one point.

In the end, George played the role as he wanted, and I always felt that, had Blake stood his ground, the movie would have been stronger. And so would George Peppard." As it was, she said, looking back, "2-E just about squeezed through as a decent part."

But Peppard wasn't the only cross Edwards had to bear. Years later the director spoke grimly of how Hepburn's performance, in the early days of shooting, was being influenced by somebody other than he. "We'd rehearse, then she'd come in the next morning and do something totally different," he said. Edwards didn't name any names, but it's clear to whom he was referring.

Before *Breakfast at Tiffany's*, there had been difficulties about Hepburn's reliance on her husband's judgement. Multi-talented, hyperactive, and, by inclination, a producer or director as much as an actor, Ferrer seemed to his old friend Patricia Neal "great fun." But he could not accept that Hepburn's performances were not really his business. As her long-time publicist Henry Rogers explains, "During the years she was married to Mel, she was Trilby to his Svengali." Soon after *Breakfast at Tiffany's*, the discord with Ferrer caused Rogers to leave Hepburn's employ. Director King Vidor had experienced Ferrer's troublesome personality, believing Ferrer had pushed his wife into *War and Peace*. Vidor explains, saying, "I had the feeling that Audrey needed somebody to make her decisions for her. He [Ferrer] knows what is right for her. He knows how much money she should be getting. I believe he collected her salary personally."

Martin Jurow recalls trouble between veteran director Alfred Lunt and Ferrer when Lunt directed both Hepburn and her husband in *Ondine*. "Mel was completely governing Audrey's performance, dictating notes on how it could be improved. Mel's interference threatened to lead to a cancellation of the entire production," he said. Now, it was Blake Edwards's turn.

"Blake and Audrey got along instantly," Jurow said, but Ferrer "seemed more bitter than ever, often making critical remarks about his wife." Finally, Edwards took Hepburn aside and told her she only had one director saying, "He may not be the best, but that's what you've got." So either she needed to go along with the performance they'd agreed on together or he, the director, had to go. "It stopped there," Edwards says. "She relied on me from that moment on."

OPPOSITE: *Yellow cabs played a definite part in the story.*
BELOW: *Paul confronts Holly in the library.*

CHAPTER SEVEN
THE SCENES

Capote described Holly's apartment as being filled with "crates and suitcases, everything packed and ready to go, like the belongings of a criminal who feels the law not far behind." Holly's apartment in the movie is much the same; its best-known item of furniture is the sawn-in-half bathtub that doubles as a sofa. Axelrod's script described a refrigerator with, inside it, a container of milk, a bottle of champagne, some penicillin nose drops, and a pair of ballet slippers. We no longer get to see inside the refrigerator, but the ballet slippers made it into the film, along with the empty bookcase and the suitcases, which contrast so poignantly with the order and security of Tiffany's. As Holly explains:

> "It [Tiffany's] calms me down right away. The quietness and the proud look of it. Nothing very bad could happen to you there. Not with those kind men in their nice suits, and all the solid silver wedding presents waiting there so patiently for someone to propose . . ."

The writer's apartment in Capote's novella is a single room "crowded with attic furniture." When it came to the movie, by contrast, according to Paramount, "art director Roland Anderson had the task of creating an apartment for a 'kept' man . . . an apartment of such brilliant bad taste that it has become a collector's item for people who like to stare."

Axelrod wrote a scene in which 2-E proudly shows Paul around the apartment, promising him clothes to fill the empty closets, but it never made it into the finished movie. Throughout the movie we see enough of Paul's apartment, with its flocked wallpaper and fake portraits, to see that he, like Holly, is in some sense a person displaced—a bird in an all too heavily gilded cage. (This "cage" is literally gilded: one can't help but notice the spangled gold telephone. The movie cashed in on early technology, as later seen in O. J.'s apartment in L.A., with its newfangled "executive phone" and electronic bed.)

PARAMOUNT PICTURES CORPORATION
West Coast Studios
HOLLYWOOD 38, CALIFORNIA

STATISTICAL SET DRESSING
DETAIL COST

Production No. 10372
Cumulative Cost To 10-21-61
Date Issued 10-27-61

PRODUCTION TITLE "BREAKFAST AT TIFFANY'S"

FINAL COST

DESCRIPTION	SET No.	PURCHASED AND MANUFACTURED	RENTALS	INSTALLATION	TOTAL COST	ESTIMATE	BUDGET	MAINTENANCE AND OPERATION	STRIKING
Int. Stairway – Holly's Apt.	1		12.25	38.47	50.72	33.00	50.00	36.22	7.76
Int. Paul's Apartment	2	2,390.45	757.00	517.28	3,664.73	2,845.00	2,850.00	508.09	65.51
Int. Holly's Apartment	3	1,835.29	89.43	608.47	2,533.19	2,138.00	2,270.00	1,280.11	66.30
Int. #2 E's Apartment	4	1,121.84		157.68	1,279.52	900.00	900.00	88.26	20.48
N.Y. Location	5	61.31		6.74	68.05			28.54	
Int. Strip Joint	6	135.29	133.75	184.91	453.95	795.00	800.00	220.09	128.10
Int. & Ext. Bus Station	7	373.35	280.00	523.85	1,177.20	600.00	600.00	183.01	92.63
Int. Public Library	8	1,814.45	229.00	346.73	2,390.18	2,499.00	2,500.00	96.85	249.83
Int. Prison Visiting Room	9	290.18		77.70	367.88	300.00	300.00	24.29	25.62
Ext. Porch	10			49.16	49.16			12.24	5.85
Int. 5 & 10 Cent Store	11	57.17	450.00	727.91	1,235.08	940.00	1,000.00	528.10	164.27
Int. Train Coach, Transparency	12	11.33		17.55	28.88	30.00			28.20
Ext. "21" Club	13	621.57	37.50	98.95	758.02	680.00	400.00		38.63
Ext. Strip Tease Joint	14	270.30		139.81	410.11	400.00	400.00	36.22	6.74
Int. Yunioshi's Apt.	15	549.39	223.50	264.30	1,037.19	830.00	1,000.00	59.66	55.25
Int. O.J.'s Bedroom	16	215.19		166.39	381.58	585.00	600.00	11.76	32.35
Ext. Brownstone Street	17								
Int. Tiffany's	18	25.35	819.50	274.54	1,119.39	1,000.00	2,500.00	68.53	21.03
Int. Yunioshi's Dark Room	19	111.03		12.29	123.32	100.00	Inc. Set 15	31.46	43.47
Int. Precinct Station	20	144.17		44.80	188.97	250.00	300.00	26.31	18.01
Ext. 19th Precinct Station	21	83.50		81.92	165.42	100.00	100.00		
Ext. 5 & 10 Cent Store & Street	22	7.95	200.00	199.78	407.73	295.00	300.00	33.26	33.59
Int. Taxi Cab	23								6.15
Int. 3rd Avenue Saloon	24	32.77		102.59	135.36	345.00	400.00	49.15	37.01
Ext. Street & Alley	25	223.83	20.25	254.11	498.19	495.00	500.00	138.48	152.62
Int. Stairway Holly's Apt.–Added	26			3.37	3.37				
Total Budget of Sets in Work							17,770.00		
Balance of Sets to be Put into Work:									
Int. Quaintance Smith's Apt.–Elim.							1,800.00		
Total Direct Cost		10,375.71	3,252.18	4,899.30	18,527.19	16,160.00	19,570.00	3,460.63	1,300.74
Property & Drapery Staff		x x x x	x x x x	x x x x		x x x x		Budget	Budget
								1,800.00	1,200.00

F-298—A-12

Given that so much of the movie was done in the studio, perhaps it shouldn't be a surprise that even the scenes on the fire escape were shot in L.A. The early scene when Holly clambers in through Paul's window dodging an aggressive man ("*quel* beast!") is one of the emotional highpoints of the movie.

When Holly tells Paul she's going to call him "Fred" after her brother, it is a moment, says Shepherd, that illustrates "the underlying, almost bloodstream, of what Holly Golightly is about, and I think that's what makes her character much more important than just the female lead in a comedy." It was also, he says, the chief reason they felt Marilyn Monroe wouldn't be right to play the part.

That Holly winds up clambering, platonically, into Paul's bed might, Shepherd says, "have been considered to some degree risqué." Martin Racklin, Paramount's head of production, wanted it cut, but "both Marty [Martin Jurow] and I said over our dead bodies." The psychoanalytical style of Holly's unconscious murmuring was a fashionable preoccupation, echoed in Hitchcock movies, like *Vertigo* (1958) and *Marnie* (1964).

PREVIOUS PAGES: Paul captured on screen in a writer's frenzy, and posing with Holly for an elegant publicity shot. ABOVE: A revealing glimpse from inside the production accounts. OPPOSITE: Holly leaves the prison—snatching at a cigarette.

50.   <u>EXT. HOLLY ON THE FIRE ESCAPE</u> - (NIGHT)

Now the coast is clear. Holly raps on the window.
Paul does not stir. She raps again louder. This
time his eyes open.

51.   <u>INT. PAUL'S APARTMENT</u> - (NIGHT)

Aware of the rapping at the window, Paul startled
sits up. Holly opens the window and enters.

                    HOLLY
          It's all right. It's only me...

                    PAUL
          Now wait a minute, Miss...

                    HOLLY
          Golightly. Holly Golightly. I
          live downstairs. We met this
          morning, remember?

Paul looks anxiously around for 2E.

                    HOLLY
          That's all right. She's gone.
          I must say, she works late hours...
          for a decorator. The thing is, I've
          got the most terrifying man down-
          stairs. I mean he's sweet when he
          isn't drunk, but let him start lap-
          ping up the vino and oh, golly, quel
          beast! It finally got so tiresome
          down there that I just went out the
          window.

There is another crash from below. Paul looks at
her questioningly. She shrugs.

                    HOLLY
          Look, you can throw me out if
          you want to...but you <u>did</u> look
          so cozy in here...and <u>your</u> decorator
          friend <u>had</u> gone home...and it <u>was</u>
          beginning to get cold out there on
          the <u>balcon</u>....

                                    (Continued)

Shepherd adds that it is the smoking in the scene that bothers him more today. It's true that to twenty-first-century eyes, the ubiquity of cigarettes in the movie is extraordinary. Even the elegant publicity image of Hepburn shows her with a cigarette, albeit one in a luxuriantly long holder, while, less glamorously, she later comes out of jail snatching at one in a way that could only suggest serious addiction today. In an earlier scene, Paul is smoking as Holly falls asleep in his arms; smoking again as she awakens the next morning and, in the next scene, throwing the stub of a cigarette away as he comes home to find her note inviting him to the party.

The memorable party scene owed comparitively little to Capote—or even Axelrods's script, which contained most of the important dialogue, but little of the colorful detail. This was "pure Blake Edwards," as Fay McKenzie, scion of a famous acting family, who played one of the guests, put it. And, on Paramount's Stage Nine, he filmed it over several days of real champagne-fueled festivity.

"You have," proclaimed the original trailer proudly, "a special invitation to attend Audrey Hepburn's open house, on the wildest night New York ever knew." This picture, it went on, "is everything you always wanted to do, and Audrey Hepburn's the one you want to do it with."

As Edwards, who went on to direct a movie called *The Party*, explained, "I don't even like to plan the scene in advance. When the cast is right, and the script is as brilliant as this one is, I just go on the set and do what comes naturally. The script itself didn't delineate that much in terms of party shenanigans, and that meant I had to step in. I ordered up champagne and we just really had a party. I got them [the actors] around and I said, you'll all have to try and come up with something, and you know actors, everyone was going to come up with something after that, and I just made a

selection." And with all those actors eating and drinking, it was a pretty expensive party for 1960, as detailed in the Paramount notes:

> "For six days they consumed twenty gallons of tea, ginger ale, and other soft drinks per working day, in addition to cold cuts, dips, sandwiches, hot dogs, and potato chips. They consumed sixty cartons of cigarettes. This produced smoke, of course, but not enough for Frank Planer's cameras. A bee smoker—actually the kind used by apiarists—was employed, creating billows of thick, choking smoke around the players' heads."

Neil Rau of the *Los Angeles Examiner* visited the set and described it as "one of the most expensive bashes ever bubbled up for a camera," and the guests as "charming and pixilated. All were tested in advance for good looks and conversational talent. In past observations of movie flings I have noted that directors usually crowded a room with extras and took their chances on what would happen. But not so with Blake Edwards, who is at the helm on this movie. He demanded and tested in advance thirty-six accredited players who earn from $350 to $500 a week on contract."

"Martin Balsam contributed some of the funniest lines for the party scene, and we all adlibbed certain bits of the business, which Edwards retained," Peppard told the *San Francisco Chronicle*. "Although he could have used mere extras, Edwards employed actors. It cost more but I think it's one of the reasons why it all comes off so delightfully."

OPPOSITE: *The party scenes were filmed in an atmosphere of real champagne-fueled festivity.*

61D.   HOLLY - (PAUL'S POV) - (LATE AFTERNOON)

She continues the talk. Her cigarette is now inches
away from the hat. Now...Contact is made!

61E.   CLOSE SHOT - PAUL - (LATE AFTERNOON)

Still helplessly framed by the young ladies, he winces
with horror. Conversational fragment: "Then, my dear,
it turned this strange blue color and all fell out!"

61F.   HOLLY - (PAUL'S POV) - (LATE AFTERNOON)

The hat is beginning to smoulder. All parties involved
are completely oblivious.

61G.   MEDIUM CLOSE SHOT - PAUL - (LATE AFTERNOON)

He tries desperately to move to the rescue. He raises
his hands as if to push between the two young ladies but
is completely frustrated by the fact that there is no
safe hand-hold. The ladies continue to gab: "...so
drunk that he kissed his <u>car</u> goodnight and backed <u>me</u>
into the garage!"

61H.   HOLLY - (PAUL'S POV) - (LATE AFTERNOON)

The hat continues to smoulder. A young man moves up to
Holly and asks what appears to be: "Have you any idea of
the time?" Holly shakes her head. Then she notices a
wrist watch on the arm of an elegant young man who is
passing by. He wears his watch face inward on his
wrist. Holly casually grabs his wrist and turns the
watch face up. In so doing she tips and spills the
drink he is holding. The drink falls onto the enormous
hat, extinguishing the flame. No one in the group,
including the lady in the hat, is even vaguely aware of
the little pyrotechnical drama that has been played.

"*Everyone* was specifically picked by Blake Edwards," Shepherd says. "All the extras were actors or actresses he knew, or friends. The man in the background with the [Asian] girl is Nicky Blair, who owned a restaurant in L. A. Edwards had a great eye for the kind of actor or actress to use."

Miriam Nelson, a friend who played the girl arguing with the man in an eye patch, says, "We just walked around seeing what kind of crazy madness we could create. He had the best sense of humor of any director I ever worked with." (Patricia Neal—not in the party scene—remembers Edwards making her do one scene over and over and over again "for fun. An evil part of him took over.") Nelson and her screen partner were told they were having a row, but not what it was about; then, at one point, her partner was to push up his eyepatch, revealing a perfectly normal eye. Edwards was really "just playing," she says—and, indeed, the shot is a precursor of all the visual gags for which Edwards would become famous in the *Pink Panther* movies.

Nelson, a professional choreographer, was also asked by Edwards to give an informal orchestration to the movement of the scene. "It flowed as though every step were being choreographed, and you didn't realize you were being choreographed," commented Kip King, who played the delivery boy who gets sucked into the festivity. Fay McKenzie imitates Edwards, roguishly: "He'd walk by and say, 'What am I going to do with you?' Then the second or third day of the shoot he said, 'I know. You're always laughing. I'm going to put you in front of a mirror and you can laugh your head off.' Then two or three days later, he'd say, 'You know, by now I think she might be having a crying jag.'"

When Paramount released an anniversary DVD of the film, more stories emerged about the famous party scene. Kip King remembered how Edwards would take a twenty-minute nap each lunchtime and emerge refreshed for the rest of the day. Joyce Meadows, who was the dancer in the white dress, remembers hearing the sound of giggling one day, and found Hepburn seated on top of a tall ladder, laughing at the activity below. She remembers an assistant director saying to Hepburn, "Audrey, would you get your butt down here? You know, you're in the next scene"—and her own shock at a star who would allow an AD to talk to her that way.

Sue Casey was asked to be the woman in the bathtub and, assuming the worst in the way of nudity, said, "I'm sorry, I can't do that. I'm a mother." Joan Staley, the girl in the low-cut dress, remembers how one scene featured her, fully dressed, on a bed with one man and with another tickling her foot from below. The scene was cut, but when a magazine got hold of a still, they ran it with a one-word caption—"salacious."

"The party is four or five minutes on film, but it took probably a week to shoot," Shepherd remembered, "and getting the actors up to speed each day was just something Blake could do. The result is as unique as any party scene on film." The party, of course, is broken up by the sudden arrival of the police; and the next thing we see is Holly, with Paul, making her second prison visit to the Mafia boss Sally Tomato (played by Alan Reed, then just becoming famous as the voice of television's Fred Flintstone). There is a hint of one kind of criminality merging into another—the fact that her association with the notorious Sally might come to rebound on Holly. But more than that, the figure of Sally Tomato itself tapped into the mood of the moment when the movie was made. It was a moment when concern about organized crime was beginning to replace the McCarthyite terror of Communism in the minds of the American authorities.

OPPOSITE: *Holly's impromptu cocktail dress rivals any creation of Givenchy's.*

67F. (Cont'd)

> She raises the water-glass full of whiskey she is
> carrying and drains it. There is a long, tense pause.
> She teeters uncertainly for a moment. Her eyes become
> glassy. She sways in the breeze like a field of ripe
> corn. The spectators, sensing what is about to happen,
> part, leaving an open space. She sways and starts to
> fall like an axed oak.

67G.   INT. MR. YUNIOSHI'S STUDIO - (EVENING)

> Mr. Yunioshi is ceremonially pouring himself a cup of
> tea. At the SOUND of the building-shaking crash, he
> jumps and the tea drops to the floor. Wordlessly and
> with a terrible calm he rises and crosses to the phone.

67H.   INT. HOLLY'S LIVING ROOM - (EVENING)

> Mag is flat on her face on the floor. In the moment
> of awful silence after the crash, Holly says softly:

HOLLY

> Timber.

> Holly takes Rusty firmly by the arm and leads him
> away. The crowd begins to mill around once more, all
> talking at once. OJ administers first aid to the
> fallen. Mag opens her eyes briefly.

MAG
Force brandy down my throat.

> She closes her eyes again. Jose looks helplessly at
> Paul. In the distance now we can hear the ominous
> SOUND of an approaching siren. Paul goes quickly to
> the window and looks out.

67I.   EXT. STREET - (EVENING)

> From the window, Paul sees Holly and Rusty about to get
> into Rusty's chauffeur-driven limousine. A police
> squad car pulls up. Two police officers emerge and
> question Holly. Holly points up to her apartment and
> the officers hurriedly EXIT SHOT. As Holly and Rusty
> climb into the limousine:

Axelrod's final script contained a long scene between Holly and Paul, as they returned from the prison, suggesting a dawning romance. But this never made it to the finished movie. Instead, we see the scene and hear the song that have become as famous as the movie itself. That song, of course, is "Moon River." This later scene was, indeed, the better one, since the country feel of "Moon River" sets up the appearance of Holly's former husband, Doc, and his revelations about Holly's history as Lulamae.

Buddy Ebsen was perfect casting as the southern horse doctor. There was, says Shepherd, "no-one more suitable to play a hillbilly," adding that he was "a joy to work with." But for the first few moments the movie plays with the uncertainty over Doc's real identity. The scene makes use of a sinister musical background as he tracks Paul through the streets of New York, before he begins to tell his story.

Later, when the movie came out, Peppard told the *San Francisco Chronicle*, "Some parts are story-telling roles, and some are story-listening parts. Mine is the latter. There's one scene I'm in with Buddy Ebsen, when he's explaining his life to me. I'd be dead if he wasn't so fine an actor. The sequence would dry up without his talent."

The story Doc tells Paul is essentially the same as the one Capote wrote, of Lulamae Barnes and her brother, "two wild young 'uns stealing milk and turkey eggs," and it, in turn, paves the way for Holly's later admission of uncertainty about her own identity. "I'm just not Lulamae any more!" she tells Doc through the window of the bus as he is leaving, but then to Paul, a moment later:

> "You know the terrible thing, Fred, darling?
> I am still Lulamae . . . fourteen years old,
> stealing turkey eggs and running through
> a briar patch . . . only now, darling, I call it
> having the mean reds."

At last we understand that it's not just from an old-fashioned, moralistic standpoint that Holly's life is unsatisfactory; why Paul won't be wrong in feeling the need to rescue her, even in the teeth of her determination to stick to her old ways. The tawdry glamour of her Manhattan life has been an expression not of her freedom, but of her insecurity.

As Paul and Doc sit together in Central Park, you could, on a first viewing of the movie, easily miss the scene where Paul finds the ring in the box of Crackerjacks. (Perhaps you couldn't so easily miss the fact that Doc married Holly when she was "going on fourteen"; a relic of the old South known to Capote.) Ironically, the props men had trouble finding a ring tacky enough for the scene, as a Paramount press release describes:

> "Problem: Paramount's jewelry collection is
> more queenly that Crackerboxy. It contains
> no obviously counterfeit rings.
>
> 'Easy,' said producer Martin Jurow to his
> partner, Richard Shepherd. 'Have 'em open
> up a box of Crackerjacks.'
>
> 'Not so easy,' said director Blake Edwards.
> 'See that pile of boxes? The prop men
> opened two hundred. They contain whistles.'"

The police helped to keep a crowd of one thousand people away—a challenge, considering the location. But the bus station from which Doc leaves was actually "the back lot at Paramount," Shepherd says.

When Paul takes Holly out on a bar crawl after Doc's departure, the movie's producers were warned not to do anything that would raise the eyebrows—and scissors—of the Motion Picture Association. So, instead of the stripper dropping her robe, all we see is the shock in Holly's wide-open eyes. This was a point on which the MPA had been clear—and even after they had had their say, a note before the movie's

UK release gave a warning from the British censor: "Deletions: Reel 3 in strip-tease, remove final shots where camera pans up the girl's bare legs and buttocks." But, ironically, as Shepherd remembers, the finished movie came closest to trouble with the censors for another scene entirely—the scene in which Holly steals from the five-and-dime store.

Shepherd points out that the whole shoplifting scene is another to which Edwards, helped by the ritualistic music, gives a new dimension not envisaged in the script. "That's where a director like Blake really gets his credit." It would be Hepburn's favorite scene—the one she, who never watched her own movies, praised to her companion Robert Wolders when, years later, they happened to catch a rerun on Swiss television.

BELOW: The MPA demanded cuts from the striptease, and this shot does not appear in the finished film.
OVERLEAF: The masks donned by Peppard and Hepburn add another dimension to the characters they play.

TIFFANY'S—THE STORE

Tiffany's was founded in 1837 by Charles Lewis Tiffany, scion of a family of dry goods merchants in Connecticut. (Charles's son Louis Comfort Tiffany was also an important contributor to the firm, but is, of course, better known for his glass design.) The firm moved six times from its original downtown location, winding up at its famous site on Fifth Avenue and Fifty-seventh Street only in 1940. It had become famous for its diamonds and for the six-pronged "Tiffany" setting. Tiffany's connection to the diamond world stretched as far back as 1877, when the firm bought a yellow stone, newly discovered in South Africa, for the then-princely sum of $18,000. More than 287 carats in its uncut state, the Tiffany Diamond was cut into a glowing canary-colored gem of more than 80 facets—a third as many again as you would find in a traditional brilliant cut.

Since then, the diamond has found itself displayed in many different contexts. It has been shown in Chicago and Kimberley, London, and Tokyo. It can still be seen, refashioned into a brooch in Jean Schlumberger's "Bird on a Rock design," by anyone who walks into the flagship store on New York's Fifth Avenue today. In the late 1950s Schlumberger designed several different settings, including the elaborate necklace of diamond ribbons which frame it as it appears around Hepburn's neck in the publicity shots for the movie. Only two people have ever worn the inch-square "Tiffany Diamond" Holly Golightly admires in the film, and Hepburn was one of them. (The other, a few years earlier, had been the society matron hosting a Tiffany Ball.) She would have been wearing Tiffany diamonds at the Oscars ceremony following the film's release, if she hadn't ended up in bed with a cold at the Beverly Hills Hotel.

A quarter of a century after *Breakfast at Tiffany's* came out, Tiffany's design director John Loring wrote a book to celebrate the firm's 150th anniversary. Hepburn wrote the following foreword, in the form of a letter to Tiffany's.

"You have brightened our faces with your jewels, illuminated our homes with your lamps, brought a glow to our tables with your silver, and given distinction to our lives. You certainly have to mine by inviting me to breakfast—how many people can say they've had coffee and croissants at Tiffany's—a memory I shall always cherish.

Happy birthday, dear T., with love—but also with envy—for after 150 years you don't have a wrinkle but then class doesn't age!

Your devoted friend
Audrey Hepburn"

Even when Paul and Holly order the ring engraved in Tiffany's, everything that was shot in close-up was filmed in the L. A. studio, but the wide shot of the store floor was real. Much was made of the fact that this was the first time Tiffany's had ever opened its doors on a Sunday; it had taken six months to wring the concession out of chairman Walter Hoving, even with the aid of public relations person Letitia Baldrige. And even then, Hoving wouldn't let any actors work on the main floor, so Paramount paid for all of Tiffany's sales people to join the Screen Actors Guild. The only real actor behind a counter was the man who waits on Paul and Holly, character actor John McGiver ("a comic genius," as Axelrod once said), and his work was filmed in L.A. "We couldn't have shot the McGiver scene in Tiffany's,"

says Shepherd, "because it's dialogue. We'd have needed to go back the *next* Sunday!"

In the finished movie, the day ends with a first kiss between Paul and Holly. In the next scene, Paul wakes up—alone—amid the rumpled sheets of his double bed. The fact that both masks are in his apartment (as we'll notice when 2-E dons Holly's cat mask) suggests he may not have been alone all night. There is nothing you *have* to see—the censor's corrections took care of that—but we surely get some suggestion of just how close the pair have grown. So, on the one hand, the next developments come as a shock, when, right after he's broken with 2-E and picked up the engraved ring, Paul is given the cold shoulder in the New York Public Library by Holly. On the other hand, it makes sense that Holly would react this way—furious and frightened at having for once given her heart along with her body.

Axelrod's first draft of the movie included a scene that didn't make it to the shooting script, in which a drunken Paul follows Holly to El Morocco and tells her he won't let her marry José:

```
        PAUL (to Holly)
    You're getting out of here
            right now . . .

        JOSÉ (aghast)
  This is most embarrassing . . .
  What would you like me to do?

      HOLLY (thoughtfully)
   Well . . . if I were you, first
  I'd hit him. Then I'd take me home.
```

LEFT: *2-E fails to understand the real significance of the mask in Paul's bedroom.* OVERLEAF: *Their body language suggests Paul's strength and Holly's withdrawal.*

This scene was perhaps felt to be too dramatic a precursor to that in which Holly, coming home with José, hears the news of her brother's death. In this stunning shot of Holly, she is seen lying broken on her own narrow bed; the audience senses her isolation and realizes that when Paul, effectively handing her over to José, says he tried to help her and failed, he is suggesting a deeper problem than her immediate grief.

The scene produced a flurry of press releases, several of them contradictory. On December 9, Cameron Shipp put out an exclusive statement, describing the moment when Holly hurls the lamp:

> "'[The lamp] was made of candy. It burst like an explosion of icicles.'
> George Peppard, the near casualty, looked on his co-star with new admiration.
> 'Great pitching arm,' Mr. Peppard said. 'You'd never steal second on her.'
> Miss Hepburn herself was broody, uncommunicative, and nervous before she played her mad scene. She had real tears in her eyes before it was over. She hurried off to her dressing room with only one comment:
> 'Is the cat all right?'
> Blake Edwards [...] got the tantrum in one take and was grateful."

On the same day, another statement was released, claiming that Hepburn's dramatic performance had been interrupted by a dog:

> "Miss Hepburn was called on to scream, throw things, and sob. She was in full cry when the interruption came. The dog was 'Famous,' her own Yorkshire Terrier, who normally waits patiently in the dressing room. When he heard Audrey scream he charged with bared fangs and threatening squeaks. Famous weighs five pounds, but he was coming to the rescue."

Yet another tale reported that Holly swept the dressing table clean of all objects, including the cat:

> "'Putney' went eight feet in his first leap, turned his head once to stare at Miss Hepburn in dismay, and climbed a wall. When he was induced to come down, he categorically declined to do the scene for another take. A 'Rhubarb' descendent with similar markings stood in for Putney and the shot was made."

Does the confusion spoil the magic? Or does it just show how deliberately the web of mystique was being woven?

When Holly, now decided on José, attempts a reconciliation with Paul, the script says it is a "day in early spring." The plants now blooming in her apartment certainly herald spring, and indeed it would have taken months to bring her this close to even a chaotic domesticity. But when she and Paul take to the streets together again, it becomes clear that this—the city she is about to leave—is Holly's other love story. "*Years from now—years and years—I'll come back . . . me and my nine Brazilian brats . . . I'll bring them back all right . . . because they must see this . . . Oh, I love New York!*"

As Richard Shepherd recalls, the camera panned 360 degrees—a technique that was new for the time—to take in the panoramic skyscrapers. This scene was filmed on the first grueling day of shooting, right after the sequences at Tiffany's, Shepherd says, "We broke for lunch at 10AM and moved across to Park Avenue. At 2PM we were finished and Blake said, 'That's a wrap.'"

OPPOSITE: *The scene where Holly reacts to the news of her brother's death is a visual coup.* OVERLEAF: *Audiences always gasp when Cat is pushed out into the rain.*

With his cost-conscious producer's hat on, Shepherd asked why, but later Blake took him to task for the public protest. "I know when an actor is overwhelmed and has done enough," Edwards explained. Patricia Neal has said, "Blake does the things he meant to do, but he doesn't work you to death. A very good man."

But no other scene could have been as emotionally taxing for the actors as the final one. The film's ending offers a different resolution from Capote's novella, yet the setting mirrors Capote's words: *Saturday, departing day, the city swayed in a squall-like downpour. Sharks might have swum through the air, though it seemed improbable a plane could penetrate it.* On set at Paramount, Hepburn was getting so drenched by the artificial rain that Production had to supply two portable dressing rooms—one for taking off wet clothes in, another for putting on dry garments, labeled in chalk: WET HEPBURN and DRY HEPBURN.

After Holly's nostalgic farewell to New York, she is suddenly arrested for having passed information from Sally Tomato. She emerges from jail, taking frantic puffs at a cigarette. Paul has her clothes and the cat waiting in the cab for her, ready to set off to the airport. Though many a movie scene has taken place in a yellow taxi, few have been more effective than this one, with Holly changing her clothes behind the high back of the front seat.

She puts on her lipstick as she hears the news that José has abandoned her. "There're certain shades of limelight that can wreck a girl's complexion," she says, in explanation of why, after the scandal of her arrest, she has to get away.

Paul's dialogue, as Holly insists that despite José's defection the taxi should still take her to the airport is, Shepherd reckons, the reason Peppard wanted to do the movie—and what he himself thinks the movie is really about:

PAUL
Holly—I'm in love with you!

HOLLY
So what?

PAUL
So what? So plenty! I love you!
You belong to me.

HOLLY
No—People don't belong to people.

PAUL
Of course they do!

HOLLY
I'm not going to let anyone put
me in a cage.

PAUL
Bull! I don't want to put you
in a cage—I want to love you!

HOLLY
It's the same thing!

PAUL
No it's not! Holly—

When Holly pushes Cat ("poor no-name slob") out of the cab, it was, Hepburn said, the most distasteful thing she ever had to do. "Of course, this is the back lot of Paramount," Shepherd says. "But I've heard audiences gasp when the cat gets put out in the rain."

As Holly tries on the Crackerjack ring with which Paul left her, twisting it onto her fourth finger, she gives a silent sob. The sheer pain of letting love in is written on her face. Over the years, this scene has gone down in cinema history. Edwards remembers shooting it with laughing sympathy for Hepburn, her face full of the cat's wet and smelly fur. As for

Shepherd: "I like it a lot," he says quietly. Hepburn never looked more moving; her "rat-nibbled hair," as Cecil Beaton once described it, drenched, and desperation in her eyes.

In Axelrod's script, there's another page worth of dialogue, after Holly finds Cat and scoops him up, and she and Paul agree on his name.

> "You know what's wrong with you, Miss whoever you are? You're chicken. You've got no guts. You're afraid to stick your chin out and say . . . okay—life's a fact—People do fall in love—People do belong to each other, because that's the only chance anybody's got for real happiness. You call yourself a free spirit, a wild thing and you're terrified somebody's going to stick you in a cage— well, baby you're already in that cage.

> You built it yourself and it's not bounded on the West by Tulip, Texas or on the East by Somaliland—it's wherever you go, because no matter where you run you just end up running into yourself."

But when the script actually came to the screen, it was obvious that not a word more was needed. Instead, Henry Mancini's song "Moon River" carries the emotional weight of the moment.

Late in her life, Hepburn told the journalist and biographer Diana Maychick that this was one speech she always felt "was meant specifically for me." She was thinking of her lifelong battle with her own insecurities.

ABOVE: *The three-way clinch—with Cat in the middle—has become one of the most famous in movie history.*

CHAPTER EIGHT
THE SONG

"On days when the sun was strong, she would wash her hair, and together
with the cat, a red tiger-striped tom, sit out on the fire escape thumbing
a guitar while her hair dried. Whenever I heard the music I would go and
stand quietly by my window. She played very well, and sometimes sang, too.
Sang in the hoarse, breaking tones of a boy's adolescent voice."

—Truman Capote, *Breakfast at Tiffany's*

Capote's novella was set in the early 1940s; his Holly knew the work of Kurt
Weill and Cole Porter, and especially the songs from *Oklahoma* "which
were new that summer and everywhere." None of these would do for the
movie, a story playing fifteen years later.

But at times, Capote wrote, she played other songs, that made you wonder where
she learned them—wonder where her roots lay—"*Harsh-tender wandering tunes with
words that smacked of piney-woods or prairie.*" The choice of composer for this new
material fell on Henry Mancini, who Blake Edwards had first met outside the
barbershop on the Universal lot, and with whom he had worked on *Peter Gunn*.
(They would go on to work with each other over and again, notably on the *Pink
Panther* movies.) Initially, however, the composer admitted, he found himself
puzzled by what direction to take for *Breakfast at Tiffany's*.

"It was one of the hardest things I ever had to write, because I couldn't figure out
what this lady would be singing up there on the fire escape. Would she sing
something with a blues thing in it? It took me almost a month to figure it out," he
remembered. In the end, he wrote a "sophisticated country song," expressive of the
wistful, hopeful country girl the producers were anxious to show still there beneath
Holly's shiny surface. (Famously, it is one that, by sheer chance, can be played using
only the white keys.) Mancini's wife Ginny recalled that while the agonizing took a
month, the actual writing took "maybe twenty minutes."

MOON RIVER

Words by JOHNNY MERCER
Music by HENRY MANCINI

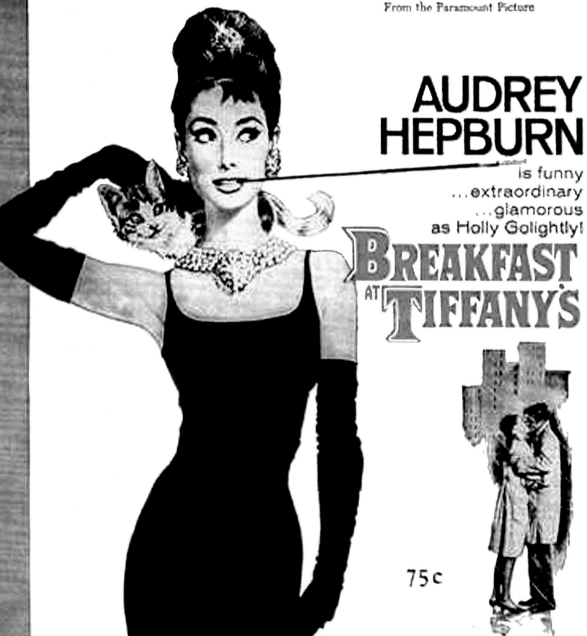

Meeting Hepburn was integral to Mancini's process. "I knew how to write it the first time I met Audrey. I knew the exact quality the song would take on when she sang it in that slightly husky voice of hers." As he explained in the Paramount press notes, when the score was published in a limited edition in 1961: "Audrey's big eyes gave me the push to get a little more sentimental than I usually am. Those eyes of hers could carry it, I knew that. 'Moon River' was written for her. No-one else ever understood it so completely."

In a newspaper article in the late 1970s, he is quoted as saying, "It's unique for a composer to really be inspired by a person, a face, or a personality, but Audrey Hepburn certainly inspires me." The music he wrote for her not only here, but in *Charade* and *Two for the Road* (1967), has, he says, her quality of wistfulness—"a kind of slight sadness. Normally I have to see a completed movie before I'll compose the music. But in this case I knew what to write for Audrey just by reading the script . . . Without Audrey there would be no 'Huckleberry Friend.'"

The words were written by lyricist Johnny Mercer, multi-award winning author of such classics as "Jeepers Creepers" and "That Old Black Magic," who himself took some time to get on message. As Mancini recalls, "When we were in recording and Audrey sang it with the guitar, Johnny said, 'Boy, that's pretty, but let's get on to something that's going to make some money here!'" But it was Mercer's boyhood memories of picking huckleberries in Savannah, Georgia (where a large river inlet is now renamed Moon River), that gave the song its particular flavor. He had, so the story goes, started a song called *Blue River*, only to discover the title had already been taken, and so fell back on those echoes of his childhood, and of Mark Twain's *Huckleberry Finn*. By 1960, Mercer's popularity, based on a style of music developed during the jazz age, had begun to falter in the age of rock 'n' roll, but "Moon River" would revitalize his career.

Producer Richard Shepherd remembers that there was a lot of discussion as to whether Hepburn's voice should actually be heard on the finished movie. There was discussion about using the voice of Marni Nixon, who would eventually dub her in *My Fair Lady*. But Blake Edwards said, "I want her to sing it, and I think she can. It's not a voice you want to go out and buy recordings of, but it's right for that song." Cecil Beaton had written of Hepburn's voice, saying, "With its sing-song cadence that develops into the flat drawl ending in a childlike query, it has the quality of heartbreak." Stanley Donen, her director on *Funny Face* and *Charade*, would say that it wasn't only the camera that loved her. "It was also the sound track. You didn't have to see her: her voice was enough to soothe your jangled nerves."

She had first worked up her voice for *Sabrina* (1954): "I had to," she said to one journalist. "When I first came [to the United States], I had no voice at all. It was terribly monotonous, shrill, and inflexible, all of which it still is, only a little less so." In *Funny Face*, she sang "How Long Has This Been Going On" in a tone all the more effective for its ordinariness. A *Time* magazine review of *Love in the Afternoon* wrote that she "even manages to sing quite effectively in a sort of absinthetic *Sprechstimme* with a tough of wood alcohol in the low notes." But she was still intimidated by "Moon River." Mancini reassured her that it had only one octave range and could be transposed down, something to which the many male artists who later recorded it can attest.

PREVIOUS PAGES AND OPPOSITE: *"Moon River," the song Holly croons on the fire escape, became as famous as the film itself.* OVERLEAF: *Henry Mancini teaching Hepburn to play.*

SS-88

SS-100

ABOVE: *Peppard takes the opportunity for an informal session with Henry Mancini.*

"There have," he said later, "been more than a thousand versions of 'Moon River,' but hers is unquestionably the greatest." As Hepburn later told her sons, "It's not just the words, but also the tune that makes a great song. It is not only what you say but *how* you say it." But her opinion was not the universal reaction at the time.

"We previewed the movie in San Francisco and went to a nearby hotel to discuss the very good audience reaction. We all deferred to Paramount's new president, who paced the room puffing a cigar," Mancini remembered. "The first thing the man said was, 'One thing's for sure. That fucking song's got to go.'" It's a story Mancini often told.

Martin Jurow describes a slightly different scenario from the famous one Mancini remembered, but anyone who knows movies can believe this was a drama with more than one act: "Audrey shot right up out of her chair! Mel Ferrer had to put his hand on her arm to restrain her. That's the closest I have ever seen her come to losing control."

Jurow remembers that when Paramount executives saw the premiere, they unanimously exclaimed, "She can't carry a tune!" Edwards left the room, Jurow stayed and argued. He would go on to wage a hard—and ultimately successful—fight to persuade the studio to promote Mancini, despite their reluctance to "treat a mere composer as if he were a celebrity."

After the preview screening debacle—after the song was settled—there was another battle. Paramount still wanted to trim the movie's score, and Hepburn sent pleading and angry memos in support of Mancini. As Edwards observed, "Despite her obvious insecurities, there was a strong core to Audrey."

In fact, as we all know, the song became such a triumph as to take on a life independent of the movie. Black singer Jerry Butler was the first to record his version, famously followed by Andy Williams. In his autobiography *Moon River & Me*, Williams describes bumping into Mercer and Mancini at a restaurant in L.A., where they had just been recording the song at a nearby studio. They showed him the music, and he took it back to Archie Bleyer, the head of Cadence Records, who, however, felt that "the kids" wouldn't understand "my Huckleberry Friend." By the time Williams was asked to sing the song at the Academy Awards ceremony a year later, he had moved to Columbia, where his new producer was more receptive to the idea of an album—"Moon River and Other Great Movie Themes."

On Oscar night the song was a hit both in the theater and on the television at home. Columbia rushed the album into the stores and, so Williams recalls, it sold 400,000 copies the next day alone. Within weeks it went to number one, and remains one of Williams's biggest ever hits. Small wonder that he later named his own theater in Missouri after the song. "I'll never release it as a single, but it has become my signature tune, the song with which I'm always identified," he says, adding that whenever he sees anyone else perform it he has the urge to jump up shouting "That's my song!" But, of course, it has since been sung by many others, including Frank Sinatra,

Barbra Streisand, Judy Garland, Perry Como, Johnny Mathis—even Morrissey. Chevy Chase crooned it in *Fletch* (1985), and comedienne Joan Rivers gave it her own mocking spin: "Joan Rivers, older than the sky . . ."

A little later, Hepburn wrote a letter to Henry Mancini:

> A movie without music is like an aeroplane without fuel. However beautifully the job is done, we are still on the ground and in a world of reality. Your music has lifted us all up and sent us soaring. Everything we cannot say with words or show with action you have expressed for us. You have done this with so much imagination, fun, and beauty. You are the hippest of cats—and the most sensitive of composers! Thank you, dear Hank.
>
> Lots of love,
> Audrey

When Hepburn died in 1993, Tiffany's remembered her with an advert dedicated to "Our Huckleberry Friend."

PART THREE: SCREENING

CHAPTER NINE
THE RECEPTION

As soon as the movie's release was announced, the Paramount publicity machine swung into action, with some memorable promotional suggestions:

> "How to make the most of the music—contact disc jockeys, ask them to play it, group all the singles and albums around poster of movie, play music in lobby during run of the movie, arrange for display wherever sheet music is sold.
>
> Guessing contest: These are not Tiffany jewels, but guess how many are in the jar and you may win guest tickets to see *Breakfast at Tiffany's*.
>
> Hire a girl elegantly dressed in a long, black evening gown to walk around town with a beautiful cat on a rhinestone-studded leash (if one is available), and wearing a rhinestone collar. Girl could distribute heralds."

But such ground-level promotional efforts were only part of the story. In a release dated October 13, Paramount proudly announced that guests "will convene in record numbers at Grauman's Chinese Theatre tomorrow night for the plush, red-carpet West Coast premiere." The list of star names scheduled to attend included Rossano Brazzi, Nat King Cole, Henry Fonda, Glenn Ford, Dennis Hopper, David Janssen, Buster Keaton, Alan Ladd, Charles Laughton, Karl Malden, Jayne Mansfield, Lee Marvin, and Groucho Marx, along with California's Governor Pat Brown. The movie's cast was to be represented by George Peppard, Buddy Ebsen, and Mickey Rooney. Guests at the after-theater champagne breakfast following the premiere were given vials of Givenchy perfume "in Tiffany bags shipped from New York for the event."

If Hepburn's name is not there, it's because Paramount was spreading its star power. In addition to the West and East Coasts, European capitals had to be covered, too. On October 19, Paramount announced that Hepburn had flown into London from Rome for the premiere. British publicist Leslie Pound remembers the occasion well. "There was this great little boy in a wheelchair, with a bouquet, and Audrey went over and kissed him." Standard practice today, perhaps, but in those more buttoned-up days, "There wasn't a dry eye in the lobby. She just had an inbred sweetness that wasn't saccharine—a lovely, beguiling personality. She charmed everybody." As he recalls, "Audrey Hepburn pushing the boundaries was the publicity. In the end, this was an Audrey Hepburn picture. End of story." That, at the time, was the movie's great strength, as audience and producers always knew it would be.

The movie opened on October 5, 1961, and eleven days later, on October 16, came the first trumpeting of a success story—a first week's "smash opening" of $178,000. In Boston a first five-day gross of $20,502 made it "one of the biggest grossers in the history of that theater," and the same pattern could be declared at other major centers. On October 23, came news that the movie had been booked for thirty more cities, and on October 27, an announcement that it had beaten the all-time record for takings in its first three days at London's Plaza Theatre. (The previous record had been held by 1960's *Psycho*, but not for long.)

On December 11, it was announced that *Breakfast at Tiffany's* was winding up a smash eight-week run at Grauman's to make room for the previously booked *West Side Story*, and the press was happy to tell the tale of a rainy Saturday night two weeks before when twelve hundred people stood in the rain to get in but were then turned away because the cinema was full. Abroad, as 1962 dawned, the picture was doing particularly well, breaking records in Rome and in Sydney.

Its appeal, however, was always going to be urban as well as urbane, and likely to play better in Paris than Poughkeepsie. In the end, the movie's box-office takings were a good rather than a great $4 million in the United States and a more impressive $6 million in Europe (where the French title translates as *Diamonds on Toast*). By the same token, the reviews were sometimes captious, but on the whole warm-hearted.

PREVIOUS PAGES: The publicity process saw Hepburn attending a charity gala in Rome with Ferrer and doing interviews in the Plaza Hotel, New York. OPPOSITE: At the London gala, a wheelchair-bound boy offers a bouquet of 'Tiffany' roses.

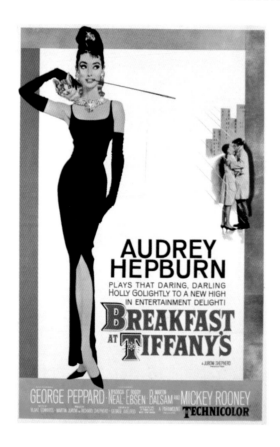

"Kept boy wins kept girl in amoral Manhattan free-spirit tale powder-puffed and purified for mass consumption," wrote *Variety* on October 11:

> "Sleek production values, bizarre story, and some topnotch acting, especially by Audrey Hepburn, make it bright b. o. contender. Whitewashed and solidified for the screen, Truman Capote's *Breakfast At Tiffany's* emerges an unconventional, but dynamic entertainment that will be talked about and, resultantly, commercially successful. Out of the elusive, but curiously intoxicating Capote fiction, scenarist George Axelrod has developed a surprisingly moving movie, touched up into a stunningly visual motion picture experience. Capote buffs may find some of Axelrod's fanciful alterations a bit too precious, pat, and glossy for comfort, but enough of the original's charm and vigor have been retained to make up for the liberties taken."

By and large, others agreed. Not, perhaps, the *New Yorker* critic, who wrote on October 7:

> "*Breakfast at Tiffany's* is one of those odd works that if they were any better would be a lot worse. It's a thoroughly silly picture, but if it weren't so thoroughly silly it would be thoroughly tasteless; a fluffy, costly, beguilingly photographed, not unhumorous but utterly false comedy, it fails on so opulent a scale that its failure passes for success. Plainly, that is a story too skimpy to yield a great big Hollywood movie, and George Axelrod, who prepared the screenplay, has apparently sought to preserve Mr. Capote by recklessly expanding him. A crucial error . . . many of his engaging wisps of dialogue have been piously retained, but in their new context they give off a downright tinny sound."

But some reviews were stronger than *Variety* in their enthusiasm. In England, Dilys Powell of the *Sunday Times*, declared, "In the Holly Golightly of print I have never believed . . . she is a sentimental fantasy . . . In the cinema Miss Hepburn with her incomparable amalgam of high spirits and delicate sensibilities, discipline and spontaneity, bewitches one into acceptance." The *New York Times* called the movie "completely unbelievable but wholly captivating. Above all it has the overpowering attribute known as Audrey Hepburn, who, despite her normal, startled-fawn exterior, now is displaying a fey comic talent . . . All the quicksilver explanations leave the character as implausible as ever. But in the person of Miss Hepburn, she is a genuinely charming, elfin waif who will be believed and adored when seen."

That, indeed, was the consensus: Hepburn triumphed over any inconsistencies. Even when a review was less than favorable, the film still ended up on top. Herbert Feinstein, for example, in *Film Reviews* called Hepburn "violently, pathologically miscast . . . [Blake Edwards] has encouraged her worst tendencies: she is so charming that both director and star should be canned and shelved." But the reviewer, whose article compared her with Brigitte Bardot in *La Vérité* as another "beat antiheroine," admitted, "I loved every minute of these terrible pictures and would not have missed either of them for the world." Who needs friends, when you've got such admiring enemies?

OPPOSITE: *Posters from around the world all presented the film's images slightly differently. The title from the Mexican poster (OVERLEAF) translates literally as "deluxe little doll" —or mannequin.*

EY HEPBURN

NEQUITA
E LUJO

Technicolor

One critical eye was less forgiving. After his initial plea that Marilyn Monroe should be cast as Holly, Capote had at first seemed prepared to accept the Hollywood version of his story. From the set, Edwards had said, "Even Capote is happy about the script. He wrote [to] the producer that we should watch the two-foot cigarette holder and not come too close to *Auntie Mame*, but he thought we had Holly right, and that was the main thing. I couldn't agree more." Martin Jurow recalls that "When [Capote] first saw our movie, he professed to love the movie and Audrey's interpretation." But, perhaps, that was before he found out George Axelrod made more out of writing the screenplay than he had the original—and before Axelrod teased him with the all-too-plausible tale that the title had been changed to *Follow That Blonde*.

Time would show that Capote never really warmed to the filmmakers' version and his opinion, if anything, hardened over time. "The book was really rather bitter," Capote has said. "The movie became a mawkish valentine to New York City, and as a result was thin and pretty, whereas it should have been rich and ugly." In one of their conversations in the early 1980s, shortly before Capote's death, interviewer Lawrence Grobel asked what the writer thought was wrong with it. He replied:

> "Oh, God, just everything. The most miscast movie I've ever seen. It made me want to throw up. Like Mickey Rooney playing this Japanese photographer . . . And although I'm very fond of Audrey Hepburn, she's an extremely good friend of mine, I was shocked and terribly annoyed when she was cast in that part. It was high treachery on the part of the producers. They didn't do a single thing they promised. I had *lots* of offers for that book, from practically everybody, and I sold it to this group at Paramount because they promised things, they made a list of everything, and they didn't keep a single one. The day I signed the contract, they turned around and did exactly the reverse."

One point Capote made, of course, does still resonate today. Indeed, complaint about the casting of Mickey Rooney in "yellowface," and the whole comic book portrayal of Mr. Yunioshi, has come to be an enduring problem for the movie. Director, producer, and casting director all lament the decision in the interviews filmed for the forty-fifth anniversary release of the movie. "Looking back, I would never have done it. I would give anything to be able to recast it. But it's there . . . onward and upward," Edwards says. But at the time, he remembers, no-one criticized it; the leading critic Pauline Kael called Rooney's role "the most low-down and daring thing in the movie."

Perhaps the most generous way of thinking about the issue is to see Rooney's role as a sideshow, filmed in a few days and curiously detached from the rest of the movie, which, as was quickly apparent, would win on its sheer style, and on Hepburn. Soon after the movie's release, copies of Holly's coat and purse were everywhere on the streets, and animal shelters reported a huge rise in demand for ginger toms. The movie eventually won Oscars for its score and its song, while Axelrod's script and the art direction were also nominated as, of course, was Hepburn, who lost out to Sophia Loren in *Two Women* (1960).

OPPOSITE: *Hepburn and Famous in their customized bicycle on the Paramount lot.*

MR. YUNIOSHI—THE DEBATE

From the first moment of shooting, Paramount press releases made huge play with the character of Mr. Yunioshi. But this was not Mr. Yunioshi portrayed by Mickey Rooney—this was the casting in the role of one Ohayo Arigatou, supposedly a Japanese comedian known to American servicemen in the Far East. Much was made of Mr. Arigatou's passion for orchids, his erratic and unpredictable behavior, his demand for billing above Hepburn's, and his desire to perform a Japanese sword dance ("with firecrackers") in the role.

In fact, of course, there was no Mr. Arigatou. In December came a press release declaring, "Offbeat casting of Rooney as 'Mr. Yunioshi' in the movie starring Audrey Hepburn was concealed for three months by studio announcements that a famous Oriental comedian named 'Ohayo Arigatou' would play the part. 'Ohayo Arigatou,' which means 'good morning, thank you' in Japanese, was exposed by a UPI photographer who came on the set and recognized Rooney in spite of his make up, which included slanted eyes, black hair, and buck teeth."

From today's perspective, it seems likely that the invention of Ohayo Arigatou was less a long-term attempt to deceive than a publicity stunt with a planned "reveal." And from today's perspective, there is little that is comprehensible about the casting or the role itself, and memories are frankly contradictory about how controversial they seemed in their day. Mickey Rooney, in his 1991 autobiography, described himself as "downright ashamed" of his role, but without casting his regret in racial terms. "I was too cute . . . and the whole damn movie was just too, too precious."

Reaction at the time was mixed. A reporter for *Limelight*, on October 26, 1961, was actually concerned to see that the same audience who accepted the sexual morality of the movie's protagonists were—being, as he put it, "apparently inoculated with the U.N. serum of love-thy-tinted brother"—audibly resentful of "Mickey Rooney's far-out burlesque." But today, Phil Lee, president of Media Action Network for Asian Americans (MANAA), suggests why protest from the Asian-American community itself would have been muted.

This was, he points out, less than twenty years after the end of World War II (the propaganda cartoons of which era Mr. Yunioshi resembles), and the internment of 120,000 Japanese Americans that had scarred a generation. "People wouldn't have protested then. It was just too fresh in their memories for them to want to make waves." The casting of actors in "yellowface," from *Broken Blossoms* (1919) to John Wayne as Genghis Khan, and on to Jonathan Pryce in *Miss Saigon* (1991), could be seen not only before *Breakfast at Tiffany's* but even after it; and it was only slowly, as a corollary of the Civil Rights movement, that things began to change. The question of the degree to which this one issue must affect our whole perception of the movie still resonates today. Some people can separate it out in their minds, and some people can't, Phil Lee says: "It's such a beloved and charming movie in other ways—and yet it's got this great yellow elephant in the room. But to me there is a place for *Breakfast at Tiffany's*. It's possible to watch in an intelligent way. Just imagine if you were showing it to someone younger. You'd explain the painful historical context, and how stereotypes prevent people from seeing reality. This is how I see the movie. I look on it not only as a movie people enjoy, but as a learning opportunity."

By the time the movie opened, twelve months after the start of shooting, cast and crew had inevitably gone their separate ways, though Hepburn and Axelrod reteamed for *Paris When It Sizzles* (1964), and there was a long and fruitful collaboration between Edwards and Mancini. The three-way alliance forged on *Breakfast at Tiffany's* would prove a successful one: in 1962 Mancini and Mercer won another Oscar for their next joint picture with Blake Edwards, *Days of Wine and Roses*. Hepburn had spent Christmas 1960 in Hollywood while she wrapped *Breakfast at Tiffany's*. Her son, Sean, was flown over from Switzerland with his Italian nanny, and Hepburn called this holiday the happiest in her memory. All the same, the cracks in her relationship with her husband were starting to show. Ironically—typically—she was understanding of Ferrer's problems. "He couldn't live with himself just being Audrey Hepburn's husband," she said. They would divorce a few years later.

That spring of 1961, Hepburn was very thin, having failed to put back on the weight she had lost while filming *Breakfast at Tiffany's*. She was working overtime to keep everybody happy. On the set of the movie, she had been accompanied every day by her terrier, Famous, but later that year the dog she adored was run over and then died while she and Ferrer were staying in L.A.

Producer Martin Jurow says the movie "brought good fortune" for a lot of participants, and in a way it's true. The behind-camera team thrived on the success of *Breakfast at Tiffany's*; Buddy Ebsen got a big break as head of *The Beverly Hillbillies* (1962) clan as a direct result. Professionally, too, Patricia Neal benefited—she said before the movie she had not had a call from Hollywood, and a year later she gave her Oscar-winning performance in *Hud* (1963). Yet Neal would find that professional satisfaction came cheek by jowl with personal disaster. She had only just finished her three-week stint on *Breakfast at Tiffany's*—"I'd been home, what, three days"—when, on December 5, her four-month-old son Theo was involved in a near-fatal accident, when the buggy his nanny was pushing was hit by a taxi, crushing his head. That same year, Olivia, the eldest of her three children who had visited her on set, died, of measles encephalitis. The only one of those three Dahl children to survive unscathed into adulthood was Tessa (mother of the model and writer Sophie Dahl).

During production in Hollywood, Neal had become close to Richard Shepherd's wife, Judy. While at a pool party, she was introduced to neurosurgeon Charles Carton and joked that she hoped he would never have to operate on her. When four years later she suffered a near-fatal aneurysm, it was Carton who lead the team of surgeons conducting the seven-hour operation. It is a saga of tragedy and of triumphant recovery that would become the TV biopic, *The Patricia Neal Story*, starring Glenda Jackson.

OPPOSITE: *Hepburn's glowing presence, at events around the globe, was an integral part of the publicity campaign.*

CHAPTER TEN

THE AFTERLIFE

In 1963, there were big plans for a Broadway musical called *Holly Golightly*. Legendary producer David Merrick had originally hired the veteran writer Nunnally Johnson (of *The Grapes of Wrath* and *How to Marry a Millionaire*) to adapt Capote's story, but Johnson gave up on the task and Merrick was forced to bring in the noted "script doctor" Abe Burrows.

But Burrows's version, too, bombed when it opened in Boston, and Merrick had to call on a third writer, the dramatist Edward Albee. The result was an extended dream sequence, with Holly born out of the writer's fantasy. Music and lyrics were by Bob Merrill, Mary Tyler Moore was to star as Holly, Richard Chamberlain as "Jeff Claypool," with Sally Kellerman as Mag. Advance sales for the December Broadway opening were higher than those for *Cabaret*. Capote had once again declared, to *Women's Wear Daily*, that he liked neither the score nor the leading lady. Nonetheless, in an uncharacteristically placatory gesture, he invited Merrick, Burrows, and Albee to what could almost be called—since Capote had relented enough to ask the Axelrods—the *Breakfast at Tiffany's* party.

All of America competed for an invitation to Capote's much-hyped Black-and-White Ball—thrown in honor of Katharine Graham (publisher of the *Washington Post*)—themed on Cecil Beaton's designs for *My Fair Lady*. "Mr. and Mrs. Mel Ferrer," as the invitation list named them, were out of town, but the masked guests who did arrive included Frank Sinatra, Andy Warhol, Lauren Bacall, Tallulah Bankhead, Candice Bergen, Irving Berlin, as well as more traditional denizens of high society: the daughters of three American presidents; the Maharajah of Jaipur; and a smattering of the European aristocracy. The party took place on November 28 in the ballroom of New York's Plaza, covered by the media across the United States and beyond. The first Broadway preview of the musical was at the Majestic Theater on December 12. On December 14, Merrick closed the show before opening night, "rather than subject the public to an excruciatingly boring evening," as he announced, dramatically.

It's true Merrick, who relished his reputation as "the abominable showman," was famous or infamous for such flamboyant gestures. It's true, too, that as a man who through the 1960s produced half-a-dozen shows in the average season, he could afford such gestures better than most. A *Time* magazine cover profile in 1966 estimated twenty percent of Broadway's workforce was in his employ. All the same, whatever difficulties the movie had had in its early days paled instantly by comparison to the Broadway show.

But no-one wanted to let Holly lie. In 1968, there was talk of a TV sitcom with Stefanie Powers—to the horror of Capote, who complained that they wanted to make "a big boring Audrey Hepburn thing out of it." Much later there was talk of a remake, with a young Jodie Foster in the lead, and this time Capote was enthusiastic. He said Foster would be "ideal." And this time he would pick the adaptor and work closely with him, "so that we don't have any misunderstanding of who this girl Holly is. She is *not* a chic or lean bone-faced Audrey Hepburn; she's a smart girl, but smart in an entirely different way."

While neither the remake nor the major musical came off, the movie's iconic status is reflected in myriad cultural references, like the song "Breakfast at Tiffany's" from Texas band Deep Blue Something, with the lyrics: "And I said, What about *Breakfast at Tiffany's*?" She said, "I think I remember the film."

The movie has been referenced in shows from *The Simpsons* to *Seinfeld*; the band "Jets to Brazil" took their name from the poster on Holly's wall, while Queen offered breakfast at Tiffany's as a lyric in "Let Me Entertain You." In *CSI: New York*, a trio of women dress up as Holly to rob a jewelry store; in *Gossip Girl*, Blair Waldorf repeatedly fantasizes herself as Holly. And that is to ignore the obvious similarities with *Sex and the City*, whose stylish heroine lives in a very similar brownstone and plans to marry in the New York Public Library, where Paul confronted Holly. In one episode of the show, "I Heart NY," Carrie and Big dance to "Moon River." In another, Charlotte makes her romantic engagement story out of the purchase of a ring at, guess where? Tiffany's. And like *Breakfast at Tiffany's*, of course, *Sex and the City* has had an influence on style and fashion that far outstrips the actual screen story.

In the summer of 2009 came the announcement of a new play, written from Truman Capote's *Breakfast at Tiffany's*, to be launched at the Theatre Royal Haymarket in London's West End. It had from the first all the potential for a major success story: an accomplished director in Sean Mathias, best known for *Bent*; an acclaimed writer in Samuel Adamson, the young Australian-born playwright particularly known for his adaptation work; and a cast lead by Anna Friel as Holly and the American actor Joseph Cross (who played Augusten Burroughs in *Running with Scissors*) as the writer.

Since the author's death in 1984, rights to *Breakfast at Tiffany's* had been fiercely guarded by the Estate of Truman Capote, which on this rare occasion gave permission, first for Adamson to attempt an adaptation and for the result to be tried out at two workshop readings, and then for the production to go ahead. They did so with the understanding that this was to be, as Adamson put it, "a new play based on the novel by Truman Capote." Not, in any sense whatsoever, a stage version of the movie.

PREVIOUS PAGE AND OVERLEAF: Mary Tyler Moore was to star in the aborted Broadway musical. OPPOSITE: Anna Friel starred in a new London adaptation of Capote's story.

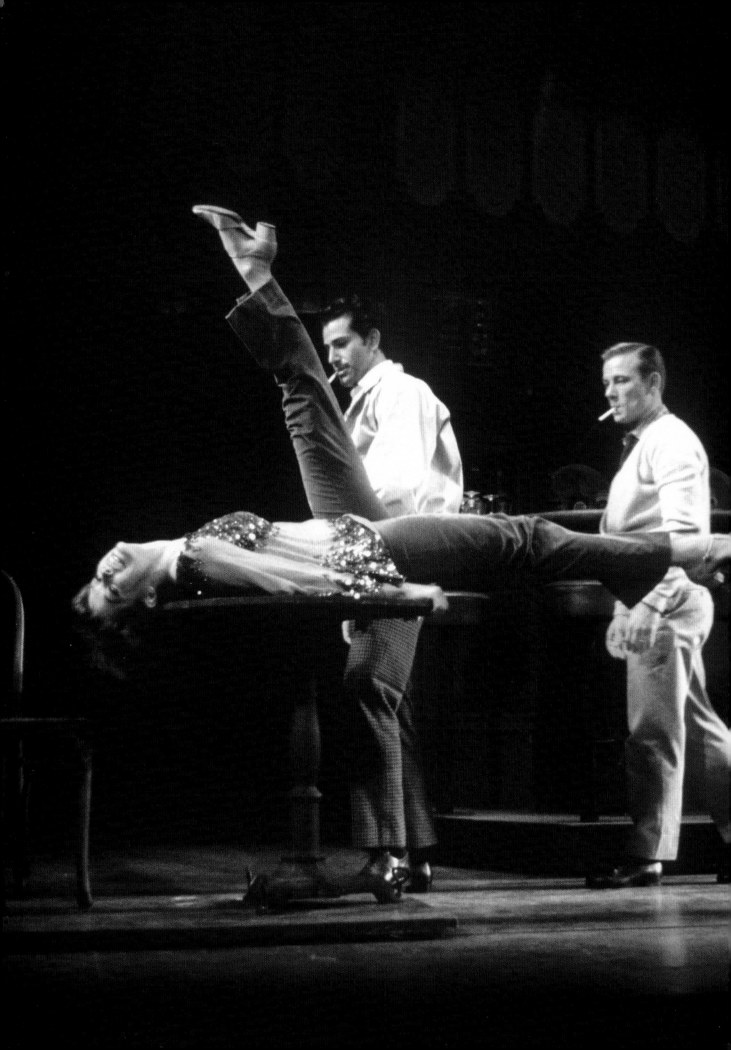

Both writer and director admitted to having been at first alarmed by the sheer strength not only of the book's reputation, but of the movie's fan base. "When I was first approached about this, I wavered slightly. I was very worried about the intensity of the iconography in our popular culture," Adamson said. Sean Mathias shared his concerns. "Can we create a play that goes back to the novel and let audiences forget Audrey? The movie is just too beloved—Audrey Hepburn is like a Princess Di character," Mathias said. In the end, however, neither could resist, and Mathias did hope that on the stage, and at a distance of almost half a century, the play might find it easier than the movie had done to show "a dark underbelly under the playful stylish mask." The journey of self-discovery Adamson wrote was always intended to develop Capote's novella in a different direction from the one chosen by George Axelrod, with his invention of a red-blooded romantic love story.

In the event the majority of reviewers were unconvinced, though they praised Anna Friel's performance as Holly—"a mixture of pluck and heartbreak," wrote Charles Spencer in *The Daily Telegraph*, with "a thrilling frisson of eroticism." The film retains its laurels: the most effective rendition of the story, even for the twenty-first century.

But even as the film was being made, the times they were changing. A new generation wanted new icons, and new moviemakers were making more realistic movies. For its audience and for its actors, *Breakfast at Tiffany's* had been a step in the new direction. The moral censorship that had constrained *Breakfast at Tiffany's* was soon blown away: Hollywood ushered in the British vehicles *Tom Jones* (1963) and James Bond; then made *Bonnie and Clyde* and *The Dirty Dozen* (both 1967). By the end of the decade, with a few exceptions like Anne Bancroft in *The Graduate* (1967) or Ali McGraw in *Love Story* (1970), Hollywood was moving down the road to boys' town in the wake of *Easy Rider* (1969) and *Midnight Cowboy* (1969).

By the second half of the 1960s, Hepburn's style of role—elegant, educated, and European in tone—was beginning to look old-fashioned. The decade gave her the successes of *My Fair Lady* and *Two for the Road*, but before it was over she had seized the chance to step back from the screen. "I had to make a choice at one point in my life, of missing movies, or missing my children," she said later. She was divorced from Ferrer in 1967, and had a second son with her new husband Andrea Dotti. "It was a very easy decision to make . . . I was very happy."

In the few years immediately ahead, George Peppard was able to some degree to capitalize on the success of *Breakfast at Tiffany's*, with films like *The Carpetbaggers* (1961), *How the West Was Won* (1962), and *The Victors* (1963). But despite television success in *Banacek* and later *The A-Team*, where he played the tough cigar-chomping commander, his later career never quite lived up to its early promise. Arguably he was a casualty of the change in movie fashion. Perhaps 1960 was too early to show that he was, in fact, the big studios' idea of a free spirit rather than anything the kids on the street would recognize as such—and perhaps too, up to a point, the same is true of Hepburn. But her charm and her stature, unlike his, were powerful enough in the long term to triumph over the anomaly—and the same could be said of *Breakfast at Tiffany's*.

In many ways, *Breakfast at Tiffany's* is a movie that should not be so adored today. Its manners and mores are long outdated, and many of us would agree with Holly when she says nobody can own anybody. A backlash against much of what the movie represented took place in the 1960s and 1970s—and yet people are still genuinely fascinated by it and by Hepburn.

OPPOSITE: *After* Breakfast at Tiffany's, *Hepburn went on to make* My Fair Lady.

A GIFT TO CHARITY

When Hepburn began the great work of the end of her life, campaigning and fundraising for UNICEF, she was, she said, at last doing the job for which she'd been auditioning for forty-five years. "When I visit sick children and then report to their community leaders or to the press, they know that I'm with UNICEF and that thrills them more than *Breakfast at Tiffany's*." But the two roles had a connection beyond any she could then have guessed.

On December 5, 2006, the black dress in which Hepburn opens *Breakfast at Tiffany's* was put up for sale at Christie's, in London, donated from the private collection of Hubert de Givenchy, who in 1995 had sold the company which still bears his name. The money raised, it was announced, would be given to City of Joy Aid, the charity set up to build clinics, schools and rehabilitation centers to help the poorest inhabitants of India.

The City of Joy charity was founded in 1981 by French writer Dominique Lapierre, after a meeting with Mother Theresa. His eponymous book—which in 1992 became the basis for a movie starring Patrick Swayze—describes the time he spent in Calcutta and Bengal, and the people he met there: the slum dwellers and villagers, and those who have dedicated their lives to helping them. In Calcutta, Lapierre would stay in the cockroach-infested shack of the Polish priest Stephan Kowalski, sandwiched between a community of eunuchs, the local gangster boss, and a leper colony.

When Givenchy offered to donate the dress after dinner with Lapierre and his wife, he was commemorating the twenty-fifth anniversary of the charity—and the forty-fifth anniversary of *Breakfast at Tiffany's*. "I see this sale as the best way to continue Audrey's wish to help children. I was sure she would be very happy," he said. In fact, it is far from the first such donation he has made. Since Hepburn's death, Givenchy has donated a number of pieces from his collection to help severely disadvantaged children around the world.

The sale estimate was £50,000 to £70,000 (approximately $80,800 to $113,000) but on the day, the dress raised a staggering £467,200 (approximately $923,000): a new world record for any dress made for a film. The last record had been when, in 2005, Dorothy's blue gingham dress from *The Wizard of Oz* sold for £140,000 (approximately $226,000). It was announced that the money would be used to build fifteen village schools in deprived rural areas. "There are tears in my eyes," Dominique Lapierre said. "I am absolutely dumbfounded to believe that a piece of cloth which belonged to such a magical actress will enable me to buy bricks and cement to put the most destitute children in the world into schools."

As work on the first of the schools got underway the following February—in Laxmikantapur, 30 km south of the city—a photograph showed an image wonderful in its very incongruity. A line of Indian children were gazing at a poster of a woman, a style, and a story that must have seemed a world away: Hepburn in *Breakfast at Tiffany's*. But underneath her image, they had pasted the words: "Thank You Audrey Hepburn We Love You."

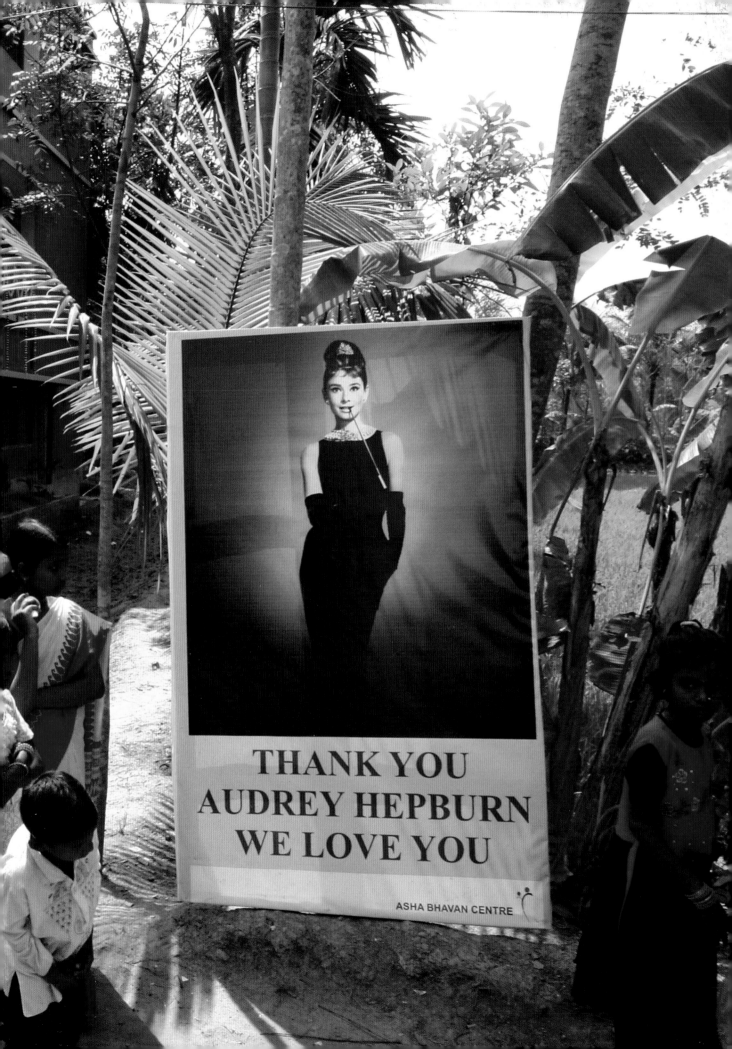

THANK YOU
AUDREY HEPBURN
WE LOVE YOU

ASHA BHAVAN CENTRE

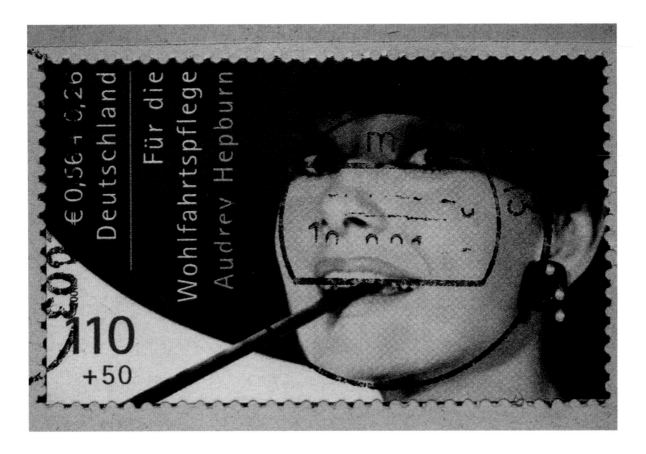

PREVIOUS PAGE: Indian children gazing at the dress which was auctioned to build their school. ABOVE: A rare German stamp, withdrawn because of concern over Holly's smoking. OPPOSITE: A publicity photograph which captures both the glamour and the loneliness of Holly's lifestyle.

Marjorie Rosen's *Popcorn Venus*, published in 1971, lambasted most of the movies and the movie stars that came out of the 1950s, from a feminist perspective. But she made an exception for Hepburn, "one of the decade's most intriguing and individualistic heroines . . . Hepburn's presence could elevate the most mundane role because everything about her worked toward a female dignity." Unusually for a Hollywood "woman's" movie of this era, this is one the rise of feminism has not damaged to any real degree.

Partly, of course, its style acts as a kind of protective shield. The lines may sometimes be of their era, but many of the clothes still look current today. Take that famous black dress from the opening shot—then, revolutionary in its simplicity and, as a result, still timeless. For her first official White House pictures, Michelle Obama chose a simple black dress and pearls, and the media at once made the connection with Hepburn.

Obama was not, of course, the first First Lady to be influenced by Hepburn's sense of style. Jackie Kennedy referenced much of Hepburn's style during her husband's presidential campaign. Like Hepburn, Jackie favored simple, pared-down shapes and elegant tailoring for public life, and in private liked sweaters and pants—a preference that slightly shocked her staff when, in 1961, the year *Breakfast at Tiffany's* was released, John F. Kennedy was sworn into the White House. More than a decade after the movie came out, when Tiffany's, unhappy with its by-then stuffy image, invited the model and muse Elsa Peretti to design an exclusive jewelry collection for them, the wildly successful line was launched with doughnuts and coffee. The year was 1974 and Peretti was friend to Andy Warhol, Halston, and Helmut Newton. What better way to introduce her hard-edged chic than a Breakfast at Tiffany's launch party?

The image of Hepburn in *Breakfast at Tiffany's* surrounds us, appearing more often with every year that passes. Holly Golightly—usually dressed in her black Givenchy dress—has been depicted on everything from greetings cards and floor rugs to advertising campaigns and umbrellas. But the modern resonances go deeper. It came out at a time when a number of women were trying to make sense of their lives and the changing opportunities presented to them, but nothing women have achieved since has made Holly's dilemma look irrelevant.

Martin Jurow describes how, at the 1991 Dallas movie festival gala in Hepburn's honor, "many women came up to tell us how *Breakfast at Tiffany's* had encouraged them to forge their own paths in the big city."

Women speak with empathy of how Holly is drawn to Paul, yet fears the idea of a relationship; how that drinking session in the bar echoes their own moments of misery. Her blend of fear and bravery, her struggle to reconcile commitment and freedom, still strike a chord today.

Hepburn, with her famous modesty, told writer Diana Maychick once, "I'm still not sure about Holly and me . . ." But she must be the only one to doubt. The film, and its sparkling, vulnerable, heroine have their own message for everybody.

Capote always said that of all the characters he had written, his favorite was Holly Golightly. Actress Anna Friel, preparing to play the role for the London production, called her "every woman's heroine." George Axelrod and Blake Edwards saw a different Holly, and then Hepburn's own magic brought its final, unforgettable spin to the story.

Perhaps that's the point about the Holly Golightlys of this world. They elude and confront and inspire and frustrate, and yet they are always lovable. According to Marvin Paige, the film's casting director, "A lot of people have that kookiness, whether or not they let it show. A lot of people want to be Audrey Hepburn in *Breakfast at Tiffany's*." It is, as Paige adds, a movie like they don't make any more. But it is also a character that will stay fresh and real for as long as there are movies.

BIBLIOGRAPHY

BACH, Bob, & Ginger, Mercer, *Our Huckleberry Friend: The Life, Times, and Lyrics of Johnny Mercer*. Lyle Stern, 1982.

CLARKE, Gerald, *Capote*. Hamish Hamilton, 1988.

CONANT, Howell, *Audrey Hepburn in Breakfast at Tiffany's and Other Photographs*. Schirmer/Mosel, 2009.

EAMES, John Douglas, *The Paramount Story*. Octopus, 1985.

EMDEN, Axelle, Yann-Brice Dherbier, *Audrey Hepburn: A Life in Pictures*. Anova, 2007.

FEENEY, F. X. *Audrey Hepburn: Incandescent*. Taschen, 2006.

FERRERS, Sean Hepburn, *Audrey Hepburn: An Elegant Spirit*. Simon and Schuster, 2003.

GROBEL Lawrence, *Conversations with Capote*, Foreword by James A. Michener. Hutchinson, 1985.

JUROW, Marty, *Seein' Stars: A Show Biz Odyssey*. Southern Methodist University Press, 2001.

KARNEY, Robyn, *A Star Danced: The Life of Audrey Hepburn*. Bloomsbury, 1993.

KEOGH, Pamela, *What Would Audrey Do?* Aurum, Press 2008.

KEOGH, Pamela Clarke, *Audrey Style*. HarperCollins, 1999.

LEHMAN, Peter, & William, Luhr, *Blake Edwards*. Ohio University Press, 1981.

LORING, John, *Tiffany's 150 Years*. Doubleday, 1987.

LORING, John, *Tiffany Style: 170 Years of Design*. Harry N. Abrams, 2008.

MAYCHICK, Diana, *Audrey Hepburn: An Intimate Portrait*. Birch Lane Press, 1993.

NEAL, Patricia, *As I Am*. Century, 1988.

NOURMAND, Tony, *Audrey Hepburn: The Paramount Years*. Boxtree, 2006.

PARIS, Barry, *Audrey Hepburn*. G. P. Putnam's Sons, 1996.

PHILLIPS, Clare (ed), *Bejewelled by Tiffany 1837–1987*. Yale University Press, 2006.

PLIMPTON, George, *Truman Capote*. Picador, 1998.

ROONEY, Mickey, *Life Is Too Short*. Random House, 1991.

ROSEN, Marjorie, *Popcorn Venus*. Coward, McCann & Geoghegan, 1973.

SPOTO, Donald, *Enchantment: The Life of Audrey Hepburn*. Hutchinson, 2006.

WALKER, Alexander, *Audrey: Her Real Story*. Weidenfeld & Nicholson, 1994.

WASSON, Sam, *A Splurch in the Kisser: The Movies of Blake Edwards*. Wesleyan University Press, 2009.

WILLIAMS, Andy, *Moon River & Me*. Weidenfeld & Nicolson, 2009

INDEX

PICTURE CREDITS

All pictures courtesy of Paramount, excluding:

Page 12: © Time & Life Pictures/Getty Images; **Page 15:** © Bettmann/Corbis; **Page 20:** © Bettmann/Corbis; **Page 22:** Photograph Courtesy of Sotherby's, Inc. "Book Cover", © 1958 by Random House Inc., from BREAKFAST AT TIFFANY'S by Truman Capote; **Page 24:** © Corbis; **Page 26–27:** © Time & Life Pictures/Getty Images; **Page 34–35:** Courtesy of the Margaret Herrick Library, Academy of Motion Picture Arts and Sciences; **Page 37:** © Popperfoto/Getty Images; **Page 40–41:** Courtesy of the Margaret Herrick Library, Academy of Motion Picture Arts and Sciences; **Page 42:** © Popperfoto/Getty Images; **Page 43:** © Bettman/Corbis; **Page 44:** © Bettmann/Corbis; **Page 50:** Getty Images; **Page 53:** © Bettmann/Corbis; **Page 54:** © The Everett Collection/Rex Features; **Page 57:** © Getty Images; **Page 59:** © Bettman/Corbis; **Page 74 (LS):** © John Springer Collection/Corbis; **Page 80–81:** Courtesy of the Margaret Herrick Library, Academy of Motion Picture Arts and Sciences; **Page 82:** © Christies Images/The Bridgeman Art Library; **Page 84:** Wisconsin Center for Film and Theater Research; **Page 85:** Photograph by Gamma/Eyedea, Camera Press London; **Page 89:** Wisconsin Center for Film and Theater Research; **Page 93:** Wisconsin Center for Film and Theater Research; **Page 114:** Courtesy of the Margaret Herrick Library, Academy of Motion Picture Arts and Sciences; **Page 142–144:** © Redferns/Getty Images; **Page 152:** © Fotoware Fotostation/TopFoto; **Page 154–155:** © Getty Images; **Page 156:** © The Everett Collection/Rex Features; **Page 157:** © Popperfoto/Getty Images; **Page 158:** (TL) © The Everett Collection/Rex Features, (TR) © The Everett Collection/Rex Features, (BL) © Getty Images, (BR) © The Everett Collection/Rex Features; **Page 160–161:** © SNAP/Rex Features; **Page 162:** Courtesy of the Margaret Herrick Library, Academy of Motion Picture Arts and Sciences; **Page 166:** © Fox Photos/Getty Images; **Page 168:** Rex Features; **Page 170:** © Robbie Jack/Corbis; **Page 172–173:** © Photofest; **Page 174:** The Everett Collection/Rex Features; **Page 177:** © Rex Features; **Page 178–179:** Bikas Das/AP/Press Association Images; **Page 180:** © Roland Weihrauch/epa/Corbis. **Jacket (front cover image):** © Getty Images

PAGE 183: Buddy Ebsen caught in Central Park, in an informal moment that echoes his role as a soft-hearted animal doctor.
PAGE 186–7: As John McGiver's salesman says, "Tiffany's is very understanding." OPPOSITE: Hollywood Agent O.J. (Martin Balsam) in Holly's apartment. The image of the stuffed bird in its cage expresses the movie's theme. OVERLEAF: Holly, Mag Wildwood and millionaire Rusty Trawler in the party scene. PAGE 192: This is the ultimate shot of Holly – oblivion, earrings, and cat.

ACKNOWLEDGMENTS

I should like to thank everyone at Anova, most notably Katie Deane, for her energy and patience as project editor; Emma O'Neill, for her comprehensive picture research; and Beverly LeBlanc, for her sensitive editing and Isobel Gillan for her sympathetic design. I'm grateful to Patricia Neal and Leslie Pound, those veterans of the 1961 *Breakfast at Tiffany's* campaign, for agreeing to speak to me, as well as Samuel Adamson, Sean Mathias, and Phil Lee. I'm grateful to colleagues like Florence Eastoe, Leonie Flynn, Daniel Hahn, and Alex von Tunzelmann for answering questions. I owe a particular debt to Christian Coulson, in Los Angeles, who not only came to my rescue by hunting up very many documents without which this book would be the poorer, but gave me the benefit of his opinions on, for example, the various drafts of the script. To all those and more, thank you!

First published in the United States of America in 2011 by
Rizzoli International Publications, Inc.
300 Park Avenue South, New York, NY 10010
www.rizzoliusa.com

Originally published in the United Kingdom in 2010 by
Pavilion Books
10 Southcombe Street, London W14 0RA
An imprint of Anova Books Company Ltd

2011 2012 2013 2014 / 10 9 8 7 6 5 4 3 2 1

ISBN: 978-0-8478-3671-0
Library of Congress Control Number: 2011923904

Publisher: Anna Cheifetz
Editor: Katie Deane
Copy-editor: Beverly LeBlanc
Proofreader: Julia Halford
Designer: Isobel Gillan
Cover: Georgina Hewitt
Indexer: Sandra Shotter
Picture Research: Emma O'Neill

Reproduction by Dot Gradations Ltd
Printed and bound in China